MEN OF CHARACTER

ONE MINUTE BIBLE

MEN OF CHARACTER

ONE MINUTE BIBLE

90 Refreshing Readings on Honor and Integrity

LAWRENCE KIMBROUGH

BROADMAN
&HOLMAN
PUBLISHERS

Nashville, Tennessee

Broadman & Holman Publishers
Nashville, Tennessee
ISBN 0-8054-2685-X

Dewey Decimal Classification: 242.642
Subject Heading:
DEVOTIONAL LITERATURE \ MEN–RELIGIOUS LIFE

Printed in the United States
1 2 3 4 06 05 04 03

CONTENTS

INTRODUCTION

The Bible, though so full of heroes and high drama, is not above pointing out that Moses had his doubts, Peter had his faults, and David had his Bathsheba.

Yet we also read that Moses had his Red Sea, Peter had his Pentecost, and David had his Goliath. These men of clay became men of character—as God worked through the ten toes and ten fingers of ordinary guys like you and me, and created men he could use to lead nations, champion holiness, and change history.

It can happen. Really.

It starts with men like us who are serious about submitting to God, men who have had enough of sin's deception, men who are hungry to see what God could do if he had every muscle and molecule of our will at his disposal.

I pray that you'll enter this book with a deep desire to learn from the real people and personalities of the Bible, to be changed by their faith and instructed by their failings, to become the newest weapon in the hand of God, and to let him aim you at the center of his will—where your life can be its best, and where your character can truly change the world you live in.

Whatever was written before was written for our instruction,
so that through our endurance and through the encouragement
of the Scriptures we may have hope.

Romans 15:4

NOAH
RIGHTEOUS IN HIS GENERATION

SELECTIONS FROM GENESIS 6 & 7

Ever think the times couldn't get any worse? Believe it or not, they have been. When God singled out Noah to help keep human history afloat, He was asking him to be obedient in a world where everyone— everyone!— was "evil all the time." Check out Noah's lonely walk.

The LORD saw that man's wickedness was widespread on the earth and that every scheme his mind thought of was nothing but evil all the time. . . . Noah, however, found favor in the eyes of the LORD. . . . Noah was a righteous man, blameless among his contemporaries; Noah walked with God. . . .

Now the earth was corrupt in God's sight, and the earth was filled with violence . . . God said to Noah, "I have decided to put an end to all flesh, for the earth is filled with violence because of them. . . . But I will establish My covenant with you, and you will enter the ark with your sons, your wife, and your sons' wives. . . . for I have seen that you alone are righteous before Me in this generation."

If we're not careful, we can almost forget that Bible heroes like Noah were real. When Noah was faithfully building a boat longer than a football field, he had no idea his face would one day be on everything from weather vanes to wallpaper. Still, he preached God's grace against impending doom for 120 years without a single convert, wiping his neighbors' spit from his face for insinuating *they* were the ones who needed help. A superman would have made it look easy. It took an ordinary man to make it look like God.

LOOK AT IT THIS WAY

These days of darkness are also days of opportunity. But what makes them days of opportunity is the power of light—of good ideas and good people—to pierce and dispel the darkness. Our cultural crisis is at the same time a cultural opportunity.

Jesus said of himself, "I am the light of the world" (John 8:12, NIV). Amazingly, he also said, "You are the light of the world. A city on a hill cannot be hidden" (Matthew 5:14, NIV). Of course, our light is totally dependent on his. He is "the true light that gives light to every man" (John 1:9, NIV). As Christians concerned about our culture (as all should be), we must ask ourselves, "How can I make the most of the opportunity that is before me to shine as Jesus would? How can I best treat the present crisis as an opportunity, and focus my beam into the present darkness?"

It needs to be said continually: the first task of every Christian is to be like Jesus. We are to give ourselves wholly to the pursuit of Christlikeness. We dare not urge in public life what our private lives deny.

—Lawrence F. Burtoft

ASK YOURSELF WHEN YOU'LL FINALLY BE READY TO FORSAKE EVERYTHING THAT KEEPS YOU FROM BEING FAITHFUL TO GOD'S CALLING. IF NOT NOW, WHEN?

ABRAHAM
CHOOSING PEACE

SELECTIONS FROM GENESIS 13

If anyone had earned the best land, Abraham had. He was the one who had turned his back on everything, pursuing the voice of God no matter the cost. Lot was just along for the ride. But when it became apparent that someone had to give, Abraham took the high moral ground.

> Abram was very wealthy in livestock, silver, and gold. . . . Lot, who was traveling with Abram, also had flocks, herds and tents. But the land was unable to support them as long as they stayed together, for they had so many possessions that they could not stay together, and there was quarreling between the herdsmen of Abram's livestock and the herdsmen of Lot's livestock. . . .
>
> Then Abram said to Lot, "Please, let's not have quarreling between you and me, or between your herdsmen and my herdsmen, since we are relatives. Isn't the whole land before you? Separate from me: if you go to the left, I will go to the right; if you go to the right, I will go to the left."

We fuss at our children for wanting their way, for fighting over who gets to play with the black-haired baby doll or the toy car with the green racing stripes. But some people never outgrow wanting things to go their way, and none of us do without a struggle. Next time you see a child ruining his whole day over something that seems insignificant, think about the things you lock horns over—a parking space, an undercooked steak, a referee's whistle—and see if a more peaceable response wouldn't look a lot more grown-up.

LOOK AT IT THIS WAY

As soon as you begin to live the life of faith in God, fascinating and luxurious prospects will open up before you, and these things are yours by right; but if you are living the life of faith, you will exercise your right to waive your rights and let God choose for you. ✳

God sometimes allows you to get into a place of testing where your own welfare would be the right and proper thing to consider if you were not living a life of faith; but if you are, you will joyfully waive your right and leave God to choose for you.

Whenever right is made the guidance in the life, it will blunt the spiritual insight. The great enemy of the life of faith in God is not sin, but the good which is not good enough. The good is always the enemy of the best. It would seem the wisest thing in the world for Abraham to choose; it was his right, and the people around would consider him a fool for not choosing. Many of us do not go on spiritually because we prefer to choose what is right instead of relying on God to choose for us. We have to learn to walk according to the standard which has its eye on God.

—*Oswald Chambers*

WHEN YOU REACH AN IMPASSE WITH SOMEONE, CHOOSE THE WAY OF PEACE RATHER THAN PRIVILEGE. YOU'LL LEARN FIRSTHAND WHAT CHRIST MEANT WHEN HE SAID, "BLESSED ARE THE PEACEMAKERS."

ABRAHAM
INTERCEDING FOR OTHERS

SELECTIONS FROM GENESIS 18

Lot had done Abraham dirty. And now he was paying for it. The pastures that had looked so green from a distance had hidden dark, ugly corners of sin and perversion. Abraham had good reason to say good riddance. But love and loyalty dropped him to his knees.

The LORD said, "The outcry against Sodom and Gomorrah is immense, and their sin is extremely serious. I will go down to see if what they have done justifies the cry that has come up to Me. If not, I will find out.". . .

Abraham stepped forward and said, "Will You really sweep away the righteous with the wicked? What if there are 50 righteous people in the city. . . . Suppose the righteous lack five. Will you destroy the whole city for lack of five?. . . Suppose 40 are found there? . . . Suppose 30 are found there? . . . Suppose 20 are found there? . . . Suppose 10 are found there?"

He answered, "I will not destroy it on account of 10."

Abraham's prayer proves two very important things. First, we can feel absolute freedom in God's presence. Prayer is a place where we're welcome for as long as we like, where we're never an annoyance or bother. It's where God wants us to be. And second, we can expect an answer from him. Even when our prayers seem to clank against an iron sky and thud untouched at our feet, we can be sure we haven't been dismissed or ignored. Like a clock, God's movements are often undetected, but they're always right on time.

LOOK AT IT THIS WAY

What a mystery of glory there is in prayer! On the one hand, we see God in his holiness and love and power waiting, longing to bless man; and on the other, sinful man on the other end of the scale, bringing down from God by prayer the very life and love of heaven to dwell in his heart.

But how much greater the glory of intercession when a man makes bold to say to God what he desires for others, and seeks to bring down on one soul, or hundreds and thousands, the power of the eternal life with all its blessings.

Would one not say that this is the holiest exercise of our boldness as God's children, the highest privilege and enjoyment connected with our communion with God—the power of being used by God as instruments for his great work of making men his habitation and showing forth his glory? It is when Christians aim at all being bound together to the throne of God, by an unceasing devotion to Jesus Christ, that the church will put on her beautiful garments, and put on her strength, too, and overcome the world.

—Andrew Murray

THINK OF SOMEONE YOU KNOW WHO'S HURTING, WHO REALLY NEEDS GOD'S HELP. CARVE SOME TIME OUT OF YOUR DAY TO PLEAD WITH GOD FOR THAT PERSON. IT'LL DO MORE THAN YOU KNOW.

ABRAHAM
UP TO THE TEST

SELECTIONS FROM GENESIS 22

Just when we think we have God figured out, just when our future seems to stretch out before us with perfect predictability, that's when God has a way of pressing a new wrinkle into our neat, ironed-out ideas. Like the time he told Abraham that A+B equaled . . . WHAT?!?

"only son" "

"Abraham! . . . Take your son, your only son Isaac, whom you love, go to the land of Moriah, and offer him there as a burnt offering on one of the mountains I will tell you about."

When they arrived at the place . . . Abraham built the altar there and arranged the wood. He bound his son Isaac and placed him on the altar, on top of the wood. Then Abraham reached out and took the knife to slaughter his son.

But the Angel of the LORD called to him from heaven and said, "Abraham! Abraham! . . . Do not lay a hand on the boy or do anything to him. For now I know that you fear God, since you have not withheld your only son from Me."

Abraham's testing foreshadowed the key event on which all Christianity turns—the atoning death of Jesus Christ—when the Lamb of God was provided as the substitute for the sins of the world. In the same way, God often has more than just us in mind when he allows difficult seasons to move into our lives. He also has his eye on our unbelieving coworkers, our doubting relatives, our faltering friends. Our testimony through tough times may be the way God has chosen to speak so that those around us will listen.

LOOK AT IT THIS WAY

Abraham loved God. But he also loved Isaac, the child of promise. This young lad had become the center of his life. Perhaps at this moment in his experience, if he were asked whom he loved more—Isaac or God—it may have been difficult for him to answer.

Get the picture? God tested Abraham in the most emotionally sensitive area of his life. Was he willing to put his Lord before Isaac? Was he willing to obey God rather than following his own desires?

You, of course, know what happened. Abraham passed the test. His love for God was stronger than his love for Isaac. He demonstrated this love through unwavering trust and confidence in his heavenly Father.

Today God often tests us in these sensitive areas of our lives. What is most important to us? Where does our security lie? We mustn't be surprised if we're suddenly confronted with a choice between our dearest possessions and the God we also love. It's in moments like these that we begin to understand how deep our love for God really is—or isn't.

—*Gene Getz*

SUBMITTING TO GOD'S TESTING, EVEN IF IT'S SOMETHING YOU'VE SORT OF BROUGHT ON YOURSELF, IS ALWAYS THE SHORTEST WAY TO RECLAIMING YOUR PEACE, STEADYING YOUR COURSE, BECOMING MORE LIKE CHRIST.

ISAAC
A LIFESTYLE OF PRAYER

SELECTIONS FROM GENESIS 24 & 25

There's not a lot said about Isaac in the Bible. He's remembered more for being a child on his way to the chopping block and an old man conned by his conniving son. But look closer and you'll see another side of his character—a man in the habit of communing with God.

a father conned by his conniving son

Married at forty

In the early evening, Isaac went out to walk in the field, and looking up, he saw camels coming. Rebekah looked up, and when she saw Isaac, she got down from her camel and asked the servant, "Who is that man in the field coming to meet us?" The servant answered, "It is my master." So she took her veil and covered herself. Then the servant told Isaac everything he had done. . . .

Isaac was 40 years old when he took as his wife Rebekah, daughter of Bethuel the Aramean from Paddan-aram, and sister of Laban the Aramean. Isaac prayed to the Lord on behalf of his wife because she was barren. The Lord heard his prayer, and his wife Rebekah conceived.

A friend of mine once advised me to be careful who I talked to when I was by myself—in the car, behind the lawn mower, through the wakeful hours of the night. Lots of us spend these dead-air times trying to solve our work problems, or worrying about how to pay for a new transmission, or winning imaginary arguments with our wife. Wouldn't that time be a lot better spent if instead of talking to ourselves, we were praying to our Father for help, getting his wise advice on the matter, and letting him sweat the details?

LOOK AT IT THIS WAY

Years ago, while Jimmy Carter campaigned for the presidency of the United States, he became the butt of innumerable jokes about his spiritual life. Responding to a reporter's question about his prayer life, candidate Carter explained that he prayed all the time. He spoke of praying while waiting for a traffic light to change, while walking, and during all kinds of other engagements. Many members of the media judged Carter's comments to be hilarious, if not ridiculous. Scores of people read his comments about prayer and laughed. But Jimmy Carter's revelation about his personal prayer life provided an excellent insight into the meaning of God's expectation of all of us—that we pray persistently.

A lot of people declare that they pray when they feel like it or really want to. At other times, they don't bother themselves with it. We can no more discard praying because we are not in the mood than we can stop breathing because we don't feel like making the effort. Regular communication with God is a basic necessity in the lives of all who love God.

—C. Welton Gaddy

MAKE YOUR FIRST CONSCIOUS THOUGHT OF THE DAY A WORD OF PRAISE TO GOD, AND COMMIT YOURSELF TO PRAYER EVERY TIME THE THOUGHT OF GOD ENTERS YOUR MIND ALL DAY LONG. NEVER RESIST THE IMPULSE TO PRAY.

JACOB
HANGING TOUGH

SELECTIONS FROM GENESIS 32

Life wasn't easy for Jacob. Confused by his mother, threatened by his brother, tricked by his father-in-law, he had learned his lessons the hard way. But what he often lacked in sterling character, he made up for with dogged determination. And God found a way to use it for good.

During the night, Jacob got up and took his two wives, his two female slaves, and his 11 sons, and crossed the ford of Jabbok. . . . Jacob was left alone, and a man wrestled with him until daybreak. When the man saw that He could not defeat him, He struck Jacob's hip as they wrestled and dislocated his hip socket. Then He said to Jacob, "Let Me go, for it is daybreak." But Jacob said, "I will not let You go unless You bless me."

"What is your name?" the man asked.

"Jacob!" he replied.

"Your name will no longer be Jacob. . . . It will be Israel, because you have struggled with God and with men and have prevailed."

God's choice of the name *Israel* for this patriarch of his chosen people (meaning "he strives against God") could not have been more prophetic. Jewish history has long been one of struggle and strife. Yet even though they were taken captive into Egypt, into Babylon and Assyria, dispersed to the ends of the earth and despised by those still intent on pushing them into the sea, they have remained. Indeed, the only thing stronger than Israel's will has been the God who stubbornly preserves them through time.

LOOK AT IT THIS WAY

Throughout his life, Jacob had gotten away with trickery so often, it was his standard operating procedure. But now the Lord said, "I'm going to see how badly he wants to live for me. How badly does he really want my blessing and to fulfill my purpose?" He had to wrestle for his destiny with the Almighty.

Wrestling with God will dislocate self-made plans, dreams, and desires and expose you to the Supreme Power. The mark of a real man of God is the one who walks with a spiritual limp. It proves he has been in the battle. Many Christians love to share their testimonies about great triumphs, but the Lord gets more glory when we share our struggles.

If you want to answer God's call on your life, you must pursue it with the same unyielding effort that drove Jacob to wrestle all night with the Almighty. You must desperately want the covenant that God promises to those who cling to him. Maturity doesn't come with age but with striving to know the Lord, submission to the level of knowledge he has revealed to you, and acceptance of responsibility.

—Tom Sirotnak

HAS GOD GIVEN YOU A DREAM? A PICTURE OF WHAT HE WANTS YOU TO DO OR TO BE? THEN HANG IN THERE. EMBRACE YOUR CALLING. IF IT'S FROM HIM, HE WILL BRING IT TO PASS.

ESAU
FORGIVENESS WITHOUT A TRACE

SELECTIONS FROM GENESIS 27 & 33

Jacob had cheated his brother Esau out of all that ever mattered to him: his father's blessing, his confirmation of wealth, lands, and honor. Now Jacob was going to pay with his life. But somehow God worked a sliver of love under the tough, hairy hide of this rugged outdoorsman.

Esau held a grudge against Jacob because of the blessing his father had given him. And Esau determined in his heart: "The days of mourning for my father are approaching; then I will kill my brother Jacob." . . .

Now Jacob looked up and saw Esau coming toward him with 400 men. So he divided the children among Leah, Rachel and the two female slaves. He put the female slaves first, Leah and her sons next, and Rachel and Joseph last. He himself went on ahead and bowed to the ground seven times until he approached his brother. But Esau ran to meet him, hugged him, threw his arms around him, and kissed him. Then they wept.

Jesus said that an unforgiving spirit hinders our ability to receive forgiveness from God. But—like many things in his kingdom—getting there requires traveling backward from human thinking. Instead of focusing on our own shortcomings, trying to reform them through mind games and willpower, we focus on God's forgiveness and love for us, his willingness to extend the freedom of righteousness to us. We fix the problem by fixing our eyes, our attention, our concentration on Jesus—and letting him fix us the right way.

LOOK AT IT THIS WAY

Leonardo da Vinci had a violent quarrel with a fellow painter shortly before he began work on *The Last Supper*. As he began to paint, his anger led him to paint the face of the man who was now his enemy into the face of Judas. This was da Vinci's revenge, and he was gleeful over what he had done.

But when he started to paint the face of Christ, his best efforts failed. He could no longer see the Savior he longed to honor. Through his struggle, he realized that he must forgive his fellow painter and erase his face from that of Judas. Only then was da Vinci able to see Jesus clearly and paint his face onto the canvas of *The Last Supper*.

Like da Vinci, we too have difficulty seeing Jesus clearly when the sin of unforgiveness comes between us and someone who has offended us. Forgiveness must be complete. It must come from the heart. We must put all thought of the wrongdoing from us and begin anew. That's what God does for us. That's what we must do for others.

—*Chip Ricks*

HAS ESAU'S STORY BROUGHT SOMEONE TO YOUR MIND? THAT PERSON YOU SAID YOU COULD NEVER FORGIVE? BRING THIS SITUATION TO GOD TODAY. HE KNOWS WHAT IT TAKES TO FIX IT.

JOSEPH
STAYING SEXUALLY PURE

SELECTIONS FROM GENESIS 39

His master's wife wasn't just casually flirting with Joseph. She was coming on to him big-time, flaunting the kind of half-dressed half-truths that any man with half a hormone would have a tough time resisting. But the way he played it was a pure stroke of integrity.

Joseph was well-built and handsome. After some time his master's wife looked longingly at Joseph and said, "Sleep with me." But he refused and said to his master's wife, "Look, my master . . . has withheld nothing from me except you, because you are his wife. So how could I do such a great evil and sin against God?"

Although she spoke to Joseph day after day, he refused to go to bed with her.

Now one day he went into the house to do his work, and none of the household servants was there. She grabbed him by his garment and said, "Sleep with me!" But leaving his garment in her hand, he escaped and ran outside.

The world's pleasures are nothing but slick advertising. Underneath the smile and the swimsuit is—not joy and fulfillment—but pain, loneliness, heartbreak, emptiness, and the sickening, sour taste of detesting ourselves later on. That's a strange way to define pleasure, but it's the best the world's pleasures have to offer. Your temptation to want them is really a hunger for the beauty of holiness. Living for Christ doesn't mean turning our backs on pleasure. It means discovering "eternal pleasures" from the hand of God (Psalm 16:11).

LOOK AT IT THIS WAY

It's hard to miss God's concern for purity. He demanded the use of pure gold in the construction of the tabernacle; he prescribed pure incense for use in worship; he required pure animals for sacrifice; he commanded pure hearts, pure religion, and pure relationships. In other words, the model Father communicates—in contrast to modern culture, peer pressure, and media messages—that purity is good. The model Father commands purity because purity is something he values. And purity is something he values because he himself is pure.

That's the kind of father I want to be. I want my kids to know that purity is good. I want my children to understand that purity is not something to be ashamed of or embarrassed about. I want them to reject the fascination with immorality and deviancy that their culture, peers, and the media so often display. I want them to know that I value purity, like the Father I serve and seek to emulate. I want them to see the benefits of purity. And I want them to see a godly standard of sexual purity in me.

—*Josh McDowell*

USUALLY, THE KNOWLEDGE THAT SOMEONE ELSE IS PRESENT AND MAY SEE YOU IS ENOUGH TO QUASH THE LIES OF SEXUAL TEMPTATION. MAKE IT YOUR DAILY, ONGOING HABIT TO "KEEP THE LORD IN MIND ALWAYS" (PSALM 16:8).

23

JOSEPH
AT YOUR SERVICE

SELECTIONS FROM GENESIS 41

If Joseph ever shook his fist into the Egyptian sky and cursed the God whose covenant required so much from him, you never hear of it. Surely there were moments of sorrowful surrender. But he never quit on God. And God never quit finding ways to use Joseph for his glory.

"God has shown Pharaoh what He is about to do. Seven years of great abundance are coming throughout the land of Egypt. After them, seven years of famine will take place. . . . So now, let Pharaoh look for an discerning and wise man and set him over the land of Egypt . . . and take one-fifth of the harvest of the land of Egypt during the seven years of abundance.

Then Pharaoh said . . . "Can we find anyone like this, a man who has the spirit of God in him? . . . Since God has made all this known to you, there is no one as intelligent and wise as you. You will be over my house, and all my people will obey your commands. Only with regard to the throne will I be greater than you."

It doesn't always seem like it—(God graciously hides it from us and does his work behind the scenes)—but we're never really in control of our circumstances. One violent thunderstorm, one slick sheet of black ice, one fuzzy spot on an x-ray, and our whole concept of *normal* can change quicker than a heartbeat. But circumstances are not our boss. They may add new boundaries to the playing field or throw a short-term advantage to the enemy, but God has a winning strategy for every situation.

LOOK AT IT THIS WAY

We get in trouble when we try to get God to tell us if he wants us to be a Christian business person, a music director, an education director, a preacher, or a missionary. God doesn't usually give you a one-time assignment and leave you there forever. Yes, you may be placed in one job at one place for a long time; but God's assignments come to you on a daily basis.

He calls you to a relationship where he is Lord—where you are willing to do and be anything he chooses. If you will respond to him as Lord, he may lead you to do and be things you would have never dreamed of. If you don't follow him as Lord, you may lock yourself into a job or an assignment and miss something God wants to do through you.

Your response should be something like this: "Lord, I will do anything that your kingdom requires of me. Wherever You want me to be, I'll go. Whatever the circumstances, I'm willing to follow. If You want to meet a need through my life, I am your servant; and I will do whatever is required."

–Henry Blackaby

DOES GOD HAVE YOU WHERE HE WANTS YOU? DOES HE KNOW THAT WITH ONE SPIRITUAL SIGNAL HE CAN MOVE YOU INTO THE PLACE THAT'S RIGHT FOR HIM AND BEST FOR YOU?

JOSEPH
RECOGNIZING GOD'S PLAN

SELECTIONS FROM GENESIS 45

Whether it happened all at once or gradually came into view, Joseph finally saw what God was up to in his life. Of course, it took a wicked plot by his brothers. It took some extra prison time. It took a famine. Only God could have put all of that together and made something out of it.

Joseph said to his brothers, "Please, come near me," and they came near. "I am Joseph, your brother," he said, "the one you sold into Egypt. And now don't be worried or angry with yourselves for selling me here, because God sent me ahead of you to preserve life.

"For the famine has been in the land these two years, and there will be five more years without plowing or harvesting. God sent me ahead of you to establish you as a remnant within the land and to keep you alive by a great deliverance.

"Therefore it was not you who sent me here, but God. He has made me a father to Pharaoh, lord of his entire household, and ruler over all the land of Egypt."

*G*od loves you and offers a wonderful plan for your life. It's the first of the Four Spiritual Laws. And it reveals a fundamental need in every person—to realize that God has made plans for us, "plans of peace and not of evil . . . a future and hope" (Jeremiah 29:11). Knowing what those plans are isn't always easy. God's reasons are rarely on the surface. But would we really want them if they were? Would we believe in the power of God if he couldn't perform his will through the most unbelievable of ways?

LOOK AT IT THIS WAY

Blind faith is not a biblical concept. It's not that we believe in spite of the fact that we're in an unending night; rather, we believe because we see the invisible light and are "certain of what we do not see" with our human eyes.

We trust in Someone who defines the word reliable. We can know from God's Word the kind of trials that we might face, and we can know from God's Word that he will deliver us. We can understand what God means and expects, and we can discern whether or not we're in line with those expectations. In fact, we must discern this, or we'll never know whether we're on the right path—whether we should persist in what we're doing or whether we should stop.

The Christian's call is not to blind, confused floundering, hanging on to God even though we can't know him or understand him. The call is to know our great God and Father, to understand his intentions, and—by his grace, wisdom, and strength—to walk in good ways.

To know him is to love him—and to understand that he's the God of love, not luck.

—James R. Lucas

TRYING TO THINK THE WAY GOD THINKS REQUIRES GETTING TO KNOW HIM BETTER, LEARNING HOW TO BE EVER AWARE OF HIS PRESENCE. YOU'RE DOING IT RIGHT NOW BY READING THIS BOOK. KEEP STICKING WITH HIM.

MOSES
TOO SCARED TO TRY

SELECTIONS FROM EXODUS 3 & 4

Moses had buried his zeal and confidence long ago in the blistering sands of Midian, far from the princely pomp of Egypt. When he looked in the mirror now, all he saw was an eighty-year-old waste of time and . . . wait a minute! . . . some kind of bush on fire or something.

Moses asked God, "Who am I that I should go to Pharaoh and that I should bring the Israelites out of Egypt? . . . What if they won't believe me and will not obey me but say, 'The LORD did not appear to you'? . . . Please, LORD, I have never been eloquent—either in the past or recently or since You have been speaking to Your servant—because I am slow and hesitant in speech."

The LORD said to him, "Who made the human mouth? Who makes him mute or deaf, seeing or blind? Is it not I, the LORD? Now go! I will help you speak and I will teach you what to say."

Moses said, "Please, LORD, send someone else."

Settledness is the enemy of service. When we get comfortable spending our nights watching TV documentaries or ingesting more news than we could use in ten lifetimes, God's gentle nudging for us to—let's say, call someone on our church's prayer list—is easy to shoot down. We fear those awkward pauses in conversation. We worry we might catch someone at a bad time. We might not know them well enough and come off sounding nosy. Fear comes in all kinds of excuses—and leaves us settling for much less than God's best.

LOOK AT IT THIS WAY

Want to know the shortest route to ineffectiveness? Start running scared. Try to cover every base at all times. Become paranoid over your front, your flanks, and your rear. Think about every possible peril, focus on the dangers, concern yourself with the "what ifs" instead of the "why nots?" Take no chances. Say no to courage and yes to caution. Expect the worst. Play your cards close to the vest. Let fear run wild.

"To him who is in fear," said Sophocles, "everything rustles."

How much better to take on a few ornery bears and lions, as David did. They ready us for giants like Goliath. How much more thrilling to step out into the Red Sea like Moses and watch God part the waters. Sure makes for exciting stuff to talk about while trudging around a miserable wilderness for the next forty years. How much more interesting to set sail for Jerusalem, like Paul, "not knowing what will happen to me there," than to spend one's days in monotonous Miletus, listening for footsteps and watching dull sunsets. Guard your heart from overprotection!

—Charles Swindoll

IS THERE SOMETHING YOU KNOW GOD EXPECTS OF YOU, BUT YOU'RE AFRAID YOU'LL MESS IT UP OR LOOK FOOLISH? PUT FEAR IN ITS PLACE. LET GOD DECIDE WHAT YOU CAN HANDLE.

MOSES
COURAGEOUS LEADERSHIP

SELECTIONS FROM EXODUS 14

You've seen the movie. Wave after wave of Israelites, joyfully taking their first free steps outside Egyptian bondage. But hardly were they out of town before the dancing turned to daggers— all pointed at Moses. The old coward in him had a chance to run. Instead, he took a stand.

As Pharaoh approached, the Israelites looked up and saw the Egyptians coming after them. Then the Israelites were terrified and cried out to the Lord for help. They said to Moses: "Is it because there are no graves in Egypt that you took us to die in the wilderness? What have you done to us by bringing us out of Egypt? Isn't this what we told you in Egypt: 'Leave us alone so that we may serve the Egyptians'? It would have been better for us to serve the Egyptians than to die in the wilderness!"

But Moses said to the people, "Don't be afraid. Stand firm and see the Lord's salvation He will provide for you today; for the Egyptians you see today, you will never see again."

One of the challenges of leadership is realizing that those who follow don't often see things the way you do. With the Egyptian hordes thundering on one side and the waves lapping the shore on the other, the Israelites saw a dead end. But Moses saw two walls of water and a clear path to God's deliverance. When others don't share your enthusiasm or your willingness to sacrifice for an unseen goal, do what Moses did. Communicate your vision with clarity and conviction. And trust the Lord to bring his results to pass.

LOOK AT IT THIS WAY

You cannot retreat; you cannot go forward; you are shut up on the right hand and on the left; what are you going to do now? The Master's words to you are, "Stand firm."

Despair whispers, "Lie down and die; give it all up." But God would have us put on a cheerful courage, and even in our worst times, rejoice in his love and faithfulness. Cowardice says, "Retreat; go back to the worldling's way of action; you cannot play the Christian's part, it is too difficult. Relinquish your principles." Precipitancy cries, "Do something. Stir yourself; to stand still and wait is sheer idleness." Presumption boasts, "If the sea is before you, march into it and expect a miracle."

But Faith listens neither to Presumption, nor to Despair, nor to Cowardice, nor to Precipitancy, but it hears God say, "Stand firm"—ready for action, expecting further orders, cheerfully and patiently awaiting the directing voice; and it will not be long before God shall say to you, as distinctly as Moses said it to the people of Israel, "Go forward."

—Charles Spurgeon

COURAGE WOULDN'T BE COURAGEOUS IF IT ALWAYS CAME EASILY. BE WILLING TO STAND ALONE EVEN WHEN EVERYONE ELSE HAS GIVEN UP. THAT'S THE DEFINING MARK OF A LEADER.

MOSES
OPEN TO ADVICE

SELECTIONS FROM EXODUS 18

His father-in-law was coming to town. And even though Moses had stared down a stubborn Pharaoh and had assumed leadership for an entire nation since he and Jethro had last seen each other, Jethro still saw room for improvement. And Moses saw wisdom worth listening to.

When Moses' father-in-law saw everything he was doing for them, he asked . . . "Why are you alone sitting as judge, while all the people stand around you from morning until evening?"

Moses replied to his father-in-law, "Because the people come to me to inquire of God. Whenever they have a dispute, it comes to me, and I make a decision between one man and another.". . .

"What you're doing is not good," Moses' father-in-law said to him. "You will certainly wear out both yourself and these people who are with you, because the task is too heavy for you. You can't do it alone.". . . Moses listened to his father-in-law and did everything he said.

The Bible makes it clear that Moses had great respect for his father-in-law. So even though Moses didn't exactly ask for it, he seemed genuinely happy to get Jethro's take on the situation. But sometimes, words of advice come from people we don't respect, who we don't like, whose opinions are about as welcome as a first-of-the-month plumbing repair. But our character shows through when we can see past the messenger and spot the hidden value in the message. Hard lessons can often be the best ones.

LOOK AT IT THIS WAY

Former UCLA basketball coach John Wooden is an inspiring model of personal growth. He recognized that the greatest obstacle to growth isn't ignorance; it's knowledge. The more you learn, the greater the chance you'll think you know it all. And if that happens, you become unteachable, and you are no longer growing—or improving.

Wooden kept learning and growing, even while he was at the top of his profession. For instance, after he had already won a national championship, an accomplishment that most college coaches never achieve, he scrapped the offense he had used for years and learned a completely new one in order to maximize the potential of his new team and the talents of one player: Lewis Alcindor, now known as Kareem Abdul-Jabbar. The result was that he and his teams moved to an even higher level of play and won three consecutive national championships.

If you are to reach your potential, you have to keep growing. When you remain teachable, your potential is almost limitless.

—John Maxwell

No MATTER WHERE YOU ARE, NO MATTER WHAT YOU'VE ACHIEVED, NO MATTER HOW MUCH YOU KNOW, THERE'S ALWAYS SOME-ONE YOU CAN LEARN FROM. NEVER GET TOO BIG FOR A LITTLE ADVICE.

MOSES
I'LL GO IF GOD GOES

SELECTIONS FROM EXODUS 33

Moses had done a lot of marvelous things as the leader of the Hebrews. Many unbelievable miracles had occurred at the raising of his staff. But as strong and respected a leader as Moses had become, nothing scared him more than making a move without God.

The LORD spoke to Moses: "Go, leave here, you and the people you brought from the land of Egypt. . . . But I will not go with you because you are a stiff-necked people; otherwise, I might destroy you on the way."

Moses said to the LORD . . . "If I have indeed found favor in Your sight, please teach me Your ways, and I will know You and find favor in Your sight. . . .

"If Your presence does not go . . . don't make us go up from here. How will it be known that I and Your people have found favor in Your sight unless You go with us? I and your people will be distinguished by this from all the other people on the face of the earth."

Running ahead of God is a dangerous game. It's like the sudden rush of fear and exposure a deer must feel when it wanders into a misty morning clearing and hears the leathery stretch of a bow string. What seemed normal and safe now smells of imminent danger. No longer can the deer trust the thick density of trees and underbrush for protection. It's on its own now. (Good luck.) It doesn't take a genius to figure out that running ahead of God can become a dead sprint into trouble.

LOOK AT IT THIS WAY

The people who do God's work God's way don't wait until their efforts fail before they begin trusting him. They begin their projects as dependent people. And in most cases, they maintain their dependent spirit to the end. On occasion when they do begin trusting in their own strength, God always lets them fall flat on their faces.

God will use various people and resources to provide for us. But HE is the source. We have a tendency to confuse the gift with the giver. It is easy to get our eyes focused on the provision rather than the Provider. When that happens, our loyalty and trust shift as well. We begin seeking things and people rather than God. Without realizing it, we become idolaters.

God is the source of everything you need. Your children, job, spouse, and friends are only tools he uses to meet the needs in your life. He, however, is the source. Any or all of these things could disappear tomorrow. But your needs will not go unmet. For nothing can separate you from the Source.

–Charles Stanley

TOTAL AND COMPLETE DEPENDENCE ON GOD REQUIRES A FAIR AMOUNT OF WAITING. ASK GOD FOR THE WISDOM TO HELP YOU DISCERN THOSE TIMES WHEN WAITING IS YOUR BEST COURSE OF ACTION.

MOSES
INTERCEDING FOR A NATION

SELECTIONS FROM NUMBERS 14

God's words in the following passages are hard to understand. But one thing comes through loud and clear. He's serious about sin and the stain it leaves on his name. No one knew this holy side of God better than Moses did . . . or had more faith in his love, patience, and forgiveness.

The LORD said to Moses, "How long will this people despise Me? . . . I will strike them with a plague and destroy them. Then I will make you into a greater and mightier nation than they are."

But Moses replied to the LORD . . . "If You kill this people with a single blow, the nations that have heard of Your fame will declare, 'Since the LORD wasn't able to bring this people into the land He swore to give them, He has slaughtered them in the wilderness.'. . .

"Please pardon the wrongdoing of this people in keeping with the greatness of Your faithful love, just as You have forgiven them from Egypt until now." The LORD responded, "I have pardoned them as you requested."

It's easy to look back on the failures of the Hebrews and roll our eyes in judgmental disbelief. Compared to them, we look pretty good. But realize that we're reading selected events that span hundreds of years from Moses to the judges to David and beyond. Their forgetfulness of God's provision was not always as overnight as it appears. Let's ask ourselves how our *own* spiritual history would appear if it were published in an honest manner, slanted to the side of God's holiness. We need to be praying for mercy, all right.

LOOK AT IT THIS WAY

Prayer must play the central role in any program of social reform. The Scriptures tell us that apart from Christ, we accomplish nothing of lasting value.

Our desire to see society restored in justice and truth inevitably comes down to the individual men and women who make up society. The battle in which we are engaged is for hearts and minds. We certainly have our part to play, and play it we must. But in the final analysis, only the Spirit of God can change the soul of man. Such events simply cannot be engineered, though they may be sought after with great passion.

Nearly every great movement of social reform has come as a result of spiritual revival, and nearly every revival was born of prayer. Regardless of whatever else we may believe about the church's responsibility regarding social action, surely we can agree that prayer for our communities, government, and leaders is a mandate for the Christian personally and the church collectively.

—John Eldredge

SETTING ASIDE CERTAIN DAYS OF THE WEEK TO PRAY FOR PARTICULAR PEOPLE AND CONCERNS GIVES YOUR PRAYER LIFE A WELL-ROUNDED FRAMEWORK. CHOOSE ONE DAY TO INTER-CEDE FOR THE NATIONS.

AARON
CAVING TO THE CROWD

SELECTIONS FROM EXODUS 32

It had been weeks since Moses was last seen, disappearing into the thick, thundering smoke of Sinai. People were starting to talk. Deep down, Aaron knew there was no need to panic. Surely God's promises were trustworthy. But hey, these poll numbers don't lie.

They gathered around Aaron and said to him, "Come, make us a god who will go before us, because this Moses . . . we don't know what has happened to him!" . . .

As [Moses] approached the camp and saw the calf and the dancing, he became enraged. . . . "What did this people do to you that you have led them into such a grave sin?"

"Don't be enraged, my lord," Aaron replied. "You yourself know that the people are intent on evil. They said to me, 'Make us a god who will go before us.'. . . So I said to them, 'Whoever has gold, take it off,' and they gave it to me. When I threw it into the fire, out came this calf!"

Think back to the scene at the burning bush. None of God's visual aids were working on Moses—not seeing his staff double as a snake, not watching his hand turn white with leprosy. Nothing . . . until God got mad and told Moses he could take along his big brother Aaron if he had to. *Oh? Well, that's fine then. Why didn't you say so in the first place?* Funny how our perceptions of people can be so drastically different from God's. To Moses, Aaron was "it." Big, strong, savvy. But God knew who was really the stronger of the two.

LOOK AT IT THIS WAY

Some charitably suppose that when Aaron told them to break off their earrings and bring them to him, he did it with design to crush the proposal, believing that though their covetousness would have them lavish gold out of the bag to make an idol of, yet their pride would not have suffered them to part with their golden earrings.

Some think that Aaron chose this figure for a sign or token of the divine presence, because he thought the head and horns of an ox a proper emblem of the divine power, and yet, being so plain and common a thing, he hoped the people would not be so sottish as to worship it.

The Jews have a tradition that his colleague, Hur, opposed it and the people fell upon him and stoned him (and therefore we never read of him after) and that this frightened Aaron into compliance.

God left Aaron to himself to teach us what the best of men are when they are so left, that he who thinks he stands may take heed lest he fall.

–Matthew Henry

WHO'S THE CROWD YOU HAVE THE HARDEST TIME STANDING UP TO? FOLKS AT WORK? YOUR FRIENDS? YOUR FAMILY? THE ONLY AUDIENCE YOU NEED TO WORRY ABOUT PLEASING IS GOD.

BEZALEL & OHOLIAB
EXCELLENCE IN THEIR WORK

SELECTIONS FROM EXODUS 35, 36, 39

Not all the men of character in the Bible are household names. Hidden quietly on the back side of the Book of Exodus, far from the high-speed chases and political intrigue of the first half, lie two men who get special note for simply doing their job. And doing it well.

Moses said to the Israelites, "Look, the LORD has appointed by name Bezalel. . . . He has filled him with God's Spirit, with wisdom, understanding, and ability in every kind of craft to design artistic works in gold, silver, and bronze, to cut gemstones for mounting, and to carve wood for work in every kind of artistic craft. He has also given both him and Oholiab . . . the ability to teach others. . . .

Bezalel, Oholiab, and all the skilled people are to work based on everything the LORD has commanded. The LORD has given them wisdom and understanding to know how to do all the work of constructing the sanctuary. . . . Moses inspected all the work they had accomplished. They had done just as the LORD commanded.

One look at the landscape of today's workplace, and the view is frightening. Maybe it's just our rosy-colored feelings for a bygone era. But maybe not. Quality and service simply aren't that easy to find these days. But look on the bright side. The market for excellence is more open than ever. If you are willing to model the principles of Scripture—outserving, putting others first, going the second mile—you'll stand head and shoulders above the crowd. Even better than that, your witness for Christ will stand the test of your actions.

LOOK AT IT THIS WAY

The second commandment rang like a death knell in the heart and head of Bezalel: "no graven images." He had learned his craft in Egypt, the most advanced civilization of the world. He dreamed of the day when he would create statuary that would last the ages. But now, while his fellow artists back in Egypt were pressing forward to perfection, he must stay behind.

It's over. Something in him dies. He feels an almost irresistible temptation to rebel. But then Moses says, "Bezalel, once more—only once more—you are to work. I want you to make the masterpiece of your life—two cherubim for the ark, the last statuary figures an Israelite will ever make. But don't expect human eyes to ever look upon them. They will be placed in the holy of holies, where no human eyes will ever see them, hidden in a dark room with God for all time."

Are you willing to give your best when nobody knows about it at all? Are you willing to leave your work in the holy place of God, and let God and God alone know what you've done?

—L. H. Hardwick, Jr.

CALEB
ENTHUSIASTIC AS EVER

SELECTIONS FROM JOSHUA 14

The spies said there were giants. Caleb said there was a land to conquer. The spies felt like grasshoppers. Caleb felt like making them eat one. But in the end, he and his pal Joshua were the only two left standing after forty years in the wilderness. And Caleb? He still wasn't finished yet.

"I was 40 years old when Moses the LORD's servant sent me from Kadesh-barnea to scout the land, and I brought back an honest report. My brothers caused the people's heart to melt with fear, but I remained loyal to the LORD my God. . . . As you see, the LORD has kept me alive 45 years. . . . So here I am today, 85 years old. I am still as strong today as I was the day Moses sent me out. As my strength for battle and for daily tasks was then, so it is now.

"So give me this hill country the LORD promised me on that day, because you heard on that day that Anakim are there, as well as large fortified cities. Perhaps the LORD will be with me and I will dispossess them, as the LORD promised."

There was a story told recently about a spunky Christian woman who died in her nineties. Only days before her death, however, she had sat down to map out her life goals for the next ten years. That's an enthusiasm for life that death didn't defeat but only redirected. If the Lord gives you long years, don't you hope you can keep that kind of enthusiasm into old age—Caleb's kind of enthusiasm—never losing your spark, that hunger to do more, that fire to give God every ounce without regret?

LOOK AT IT THIS WAY

Caleb is a classic example of a man who never lost his spiritual edge. Where did this seasoned veteran get his spiritual grit—his chutzpah? What made him endure while others fell by the wayside right and left? The Bible says, "He followed the LORD, the God of Israel, wholeheartedly" (Joshua 14:14, NIV). He never lost sight of the promises of God.

Interestingly enough, of all those who received the Promised Land as their inheritance, Caleb was the only one who completely drove out the enemy. He faced some of the most formidable foes in the entire land. Hebron was no garden spot. It was rugged and treacherous. But Caleb—even in his elderly years—was no lightweight. He wasn't looking for a pleasant retirement community to settle down in and rock his way toward heaven. He was looking for a scrap.

So he asked for one of the toughest assignments, and he successfully—single-handedly—drove out the enemies from Hebron. While others longed for Egypt, Caleb longed for Hebron. While others looked back, Caleb looked forward.

—Greg Laurie

SEEK OUT SOMEONE SOON WHO'S STILL MODELING AN ENTHUSIASTIC CHRISTIAN LIFESTYLE INTO THEIR OLDER YEARS. THEY'LL INSPIRE YOU TO GREATER THINGS. AND YOU'LL INSPIRE THEM TO KEEP ON GOING.

PHINEHAS
RIGHTEOUS INDIGNATION

SELECTIONS FROM NUMBERS 25

Aaron could have learned a thing or two from his son Phinehas. Faced with a similar outbreak of sin and rebellion among the Israelites, Aaron broke down under pressure. But Phinehas broke out. And his high regard for holiness gave the people reason for hope.

> *An Israelite man came bringing a Midianite woman to his brothers in plain view of Moses and the whole Israelite community. . . . When Phinehas son of Eleazar, son of Aaron the priest, saw this, he got up from the assembly and took a spear in his hand. Then he followed the Israelite man into the tent, and pierced both of them through, the Israelite man and the woman, through her belly. . . .*
>
> *The LORD spoke to Moses: "Phinehas . . . turned back My wrath from the Israelites because he displayed My zeal among them, so that in My zeal I did not finish off the Israelites. . . . He was zealous for his God and made atonement for the Israelites.' "*

Some things are worth fighting for. And our families are one of the biggest. We tend to start by bashing the media and the movies. And certainly they carry their share of the blame. But some of the culprits come in much different cloaks. Like sixty-hour workweeks that run into months. And Saturdays at the golf course (ouch, that hurt). Even church meetings that take up three nights in a row. Sometimes we've got to put our foot down and say that our family needs us more than anyone else does. It's the right thing to do.

LOOK AT IT THIS WAY

We have lost our spiritual equilibrium and inverted our values. We have ridiculed the absolute truth of your Word and called it moral pluralism. We have worshiped other gods and called it multiculturalism. We have endorsed perversion and called it an alternative lifestyle. We have exploited the poor and called it the lottery. We have neglected the needy and called it self-preservation. We have rewarded laziness and called it welfare. We have killed our unborn and called it a choice. We have shot abortionists and called it justifiable. We have neglected to discipline our children and called it building their self-esteem. We have abused power and called it political savvy. We have coveted our neighbors' possessions and called it ambition. We have polluted the air with profanity and pornography and called it freedom of expression. We have ridiculed the time-honored values of our forefathers and called it enlightenment.

Search us, O God, and know our hearts today. Try us and see if there be some wicked way in us. Cleanse us from every sin and set us free.

—Joe Wright, in a prayer before the Kansas state legislature

IT'S EASY TO SIT AROUND DECRYING THE ILLS OF SOCIETY. BUT WHEN DID YOU LAST STAND UP AND DO SOMETHING CONSTRUCTIVE TO FIGHT EVIL, TO CHAMPION THE CAUSE OF RIGHTEOUSNESS?

JOSHUA
BIG SHOES TO FILL

SELECTIONS FROM JOSHUA 3 & 4

Moses was president, CEO, pastor, judge, and ruler, all rolled into one. And his death literally took from the Hebrew people the only leader this generation had ever known. The task that lay ahead for his successor was more than impossible. Good thing it wasn't impossible for God.

Joshua told the Israelites, "Come closer and listen to the words of the LORD your God. . . .

"Look! The ark of the covenant of the Lord of all the earth is going on ahead of you into the Jordan. Now choose 12 men from the tribes of Israel, one man for each tribe. When the feet of the priests who carry the ark of the LORD, the Lord of all the earth, come to rest in the Jordan's waters, its waters will be cut off. The water flowing downstream will stand as one mass.". . .

On that day the LORD exalted Joshua in the sight of all Israel, and they revered him all the days of his life, as they had revered Moses.

Even the most progressive of us can cringe at change. Your beloved pastor resigns to minister in another church. Or your boss—(you'd finally gotten a good one)—is transferred to another state. Just when you thought things were settled again, your widowed mother remarries or your favorite neighbors move away. And someone takes the place of someone who's irreplaceable. Turnovers like these are never easy, but if your trust is in God instead of in people, he can fill your seasons of change with unpredictable blessings.

LOOK AT IT THIS WAY

Think of the temptation Joshua must have faced. How easy it would have been to draw attention to himself and to attempt to build his own ego. Joshua, primarily because of his feelings of insecurity, was very vulnerable to this kind of temptation. Fearful people are always vulnerable to pride. They often overreact to praise and honor.

Joshua, however, did not respond either with false humility or with pride. He had discovered security in God's promises to him. He was able to rise above the temptation to glorify himself. He gave honor to the only one who could be given credit for the miracle that was about to take place.

Joshua's response was admirable, especially in view of the fact that he had been fearful and threatened by this great task. But his response shows the main reason why God chose to use Joshua in the first place. He knew he could trust him with this leadership role. He knew Joshua could handle the temptation that comes to every individual who is entrusted with great responsibility.

—Gene Getz

WHETHER YOU'RE FILLING BIG SHOES YOURSELF OR HAVING TO GET USED TO SOMEONE ELSE WHO IS, YOU'RE IN ONE OF GOD'S MOST PRODUCTIVE PERIODS OF TESTING. HE WILL SEE YOU THROUGH IF YOU'LL LET HIM.

GIDEON
DOUBTS AND FEARS

SELECTIONS FROM JUDGES 7

When you think of Gideon, if all that comes to mind is a fierce fighting man, slamming clay pots and blowing trumpets, take a closer look at the material God chose to work with—a bundle of nerves whose fears left no doubt that victory came only from "the sword of the Lord."

The LORD told Gideon, "Get up! Go down among the camp, for I have given it into your hand. But if you are afraid to go down, take Purah, your servant, down to the camp with you.". . . He went down along with Purah to the edge of the troops in the camp. . . .

Look! A man is telling his dream to his friend. . . . "Right here I saw a loaf of barley bread rolling into Midian's camp. It came to the tent, struck it, and it fell down. It turned the tent upside down, and the tent collapsed."

His friend answered, "This is nothing other than the sword of Gideon, son of Joash, the man of Israel! God has given Midian with its entire army into his hand."

Remember the fleece incident? Gideon stalls God for a sign—for something that makes him feel better about risking his life in battle, something a bit more substantial from God than just his word. And God graciously gives it. Not once, but twice. He knew that this little tennis match Gideon was playing wasn't some *"Prove it!"* born of raw, cynical skepticism. It came from someone simply scared to death of what the Lord was asking of him. And apparently, God's willing to work with that.

LOOK AT IT THIS WAY

Is it a sin to doubt? It can be if unbelief encourages disobedience to God or disloyalty to life's best. Yet doubt is not all bad. Some of history's notable doubters have become agents of change, correctors of error, and pioneers of new patterns of life. Great saints of the church, like Augustine and Luther, were plagued by periods of nagging doubt and depression. John Bunyan's classic allegory *Pilgrim's Progress* reports a Christian pilgrim's tortured victory over questions and severe trials. There can be no greatness of devotion without the risk of defection from one's cause.

Faith and doubt, like joy and sorrow, together compose the life of God's people. Since commitment to Christ is a growing process, not a static experience, doubt may furnish an opportunity for growth. Personal experiences like betrayal of trust, fear of rejection, overwhelming tasks, and burdensome debts may provoke anxious concern in a stalwart heart. Doubt can destroy you. But if you learn to master it, skepticism can strengthen your commitment.

—C. W. Brister

TURN YOUR FEARS AND DOUBTS INTO TRUSTED WARNING SIGNS THAT THE CHALLENGE YOU'RE FACING IS INDEED TOO BIG FOR YOU TO HANDLE ALONE. GOD DOESN'T EXPECT YOU TO DO IT ALL BY YOURSELF.

JEPHTHAH
CARELESS WORDS

SELECTIONS FROM JUDGES 11

Let's give him the benefit of the doubt. Let's say Jephthah just got a little carried away with himself, caught up in the nervous, battle-ready excitement around the Israelite campfire. Then why, after the way things turned out, did he go through with his promise? He had a bad case of foolishness.

Jephthah made a vow to the Lord and said, "If You really do give the Ammonites into my hand, then whatever comes out of the doors of my house to greet me when I return in peace from the Ammonites, it will belong to the Lord. I will offer it up as a burnt offering.". . . And the Lord gave them into his hand. . . .

Jephthah came to his house in Mizpah. Look! His daughter is coming out to meet him with tambourines and dancing. She was his only child. . . .Seeing her, he tore his clothes and moaned, "Oh, no, my daughter! You have surely brought me to my knees! You have ruined me. Indeed, I made a promise to the Lord and cannot go back on it."

In a world where few things are sacred, God is still serious business. That's why even for believers, who feel no threat of eternal punishment, Christ's statement that "on the day of judgment people will have to account for every careless word they speak" is cause for caution and alarm (Matthew 12:36). Our words matter. We toss them around so lightly, but their weight is measured by the people they help or hurt, by the inner attitudes they reveal about us. May that day of judgment prove us people of careful words.

LOOK AT IT THIS WAY

Whatever the reasons behind Jephthah's rash vow, he paid for his actions—just as fathers throughout history have lost their children when vows at work conflict with vows at home. This story illustrates the double bind many men feel between the call of work and family. Many warrior fathers and men of integrity, zealous to uphold their work and their word at all costs, make the same mistake Jephthah did.

We can empathize with his dilemma by remembering that many fathers break promises to their family. We conveniently forget our girl's piano recital or our boy's baseball game for a "prior commitment" (another business meeting, a game of golf, or a men's night out). Workaholics ask their family to understand that work must come first. Military men put "God and country" above family. So also did Jephthah. He loved God and responded to the call of people who pressed him into military service . . . but forgot the welfare of his own family.

—Dietrich Gruen

LIKE TIME, TALENTS, AND MONEY, YOUR WORDS ARE A TREASURE TO BE MANAGED WITH GODLY CARE AND DEVOTION. ALWAYS TRY PUTTING SOME THOUGHT BEHIND WHAT YOU SAY.

SAMSON
DEALING WITH CONSEQUENCES

SELECTIONS FROM JUDGES 16

Samson blew it big time. Here's a guy with everything in the world going for him, and he throws it all away. For a thrill. For a kick. For a pretty girl. But here's also living proof that even at the very end, even at the very bottom, people can change. And God can still hear them.

The temple was full of men and women. All the Philistine rulers were there as were about 3,000 men and women who were on the roof watching Samson entertain. Samson called out to the LORD, "O LORD God, please remember me and strengthen me only this once, O God, so that with one act of vengeance I may get revenge on the Philistines for my two eyes."

Samson took hold of the two middle pillars on which the temple rested. He leaned against them—one on his right hand and the other on his left. Then Samson said, "Let me die with the Philistines." He pushed with all his strength, and the temple fell on the rulers and all the people inside.

Every picture you see of Samson is of this massive, hulking brute, carving up Philistines with a jawbone or snapping the city doors off their hinges. But if he were really some Mr. Universe look-alike, then why would his enemies have to resort to trickery to find the secret of his strength? If he were made out of muscle, then what's the big secret? Samson knew that he was only as strong as his God let him be. How dangerous it is to see more in ourselves than is really there.

LOOK AT IT THIS WAY

The end of Samson's life is a solemn reminder that there are consequences to sin. For twenty years Samson assumed he could ignore all of the secret faults that lay beneath the surface of his life, but he was wrong. He thought he could get away with a few minor indiscretions from time to time, but he couldn't. We all tend to believe at one time or another that we can ignore our sins. But the fact remains, our sins will not ignore us.

With his last burst of energy, Samson took hold of the pillars on either side of him. He was blind, but he had actually begun to see better than he had in more than twenty years. He heard the Philistines mocking God, so he prayed: "Oh Lord God, remember me and strengthen me just one more time." At long last, he realized that the strength he once possessed was not his, but God's. So he pleaded, "Let me die right here." With all of his great advantages thoroughly squandered, Samson finally began to understand: he surrendered his life completely to the will and purposes of Almighty God. Better late than never.

—O. S. Hawkins

YOU MAY FEEL LIKE YOU'VE MADE MISTAKES YOU'LL NEVER LIVE DOWN. BUT IT'S NEVER TOO LATE TO FACE YOUR FAULTS, LEARN YOUR LESSONS, AND DO YOUR BEST WITH WHAT'S LEFT.

BOAZ
A CASE FOR KINDNESS

SELECTIONS FROM RUTH 2

Old Testament men don't commonly come off as being kind. Their primitive habits and customs strike a noticeable contrast to the sensitive model of the modern man. Boaz was a big exception. His example of putting a priority on people still has a lot to say to us. Today.

Boaz asked his servant, the overseer of the harvesters, "To whom does this young woman belong?" The servant overseeing the harvesters answered, "She is the young Moabite girl who came back with Naomi from Moabite territory. She asked, 'May I please glean and gather bundles behind the harvesters?'" . . .

Boaz told Ruth, "Listen carefully, my daughter. Don't go glean in any other field. Don't even cross the boundary line of this one, but stick close to my young servant girls right here. . . . May the LORD reward what you've done. May you receive your wages in full from the LORD God of Israel, under whose wings you have come for refuge."

In reality, Boaz was much more than a kind, landed gentleman who gave Ruth the free run of his grain field. He was a kinsman-redeemer—one who by law had the right to buy the lands and possessions of bankrupt relatives in order to keep their holdings in the family. In the same way, Jesus Christ is the one who has met us in our bankruptcy and assumed the role of our older brother, rescuing us from a debtor's prison by making full payment on our rising balance of sins, redeeming us from certain death.

LOOK AT IT THIS WAY

Clemens has his head full of imaginary piety. He is often proposing to himself what he would do if he had a great estate. He would outdo all charitable men that are gone before him; he would allow himself only necessaries, that widows and orphans, the sick and distressed, might find relief out of his estate. He tells you that all other ways of spending an estate is folly and madness.

Now, Clemens has at present a moderate estate, which he spends upon himself in the same vanities and indulgences as other people do. He might live upon one-third of his fortune and make the rest the support of the poor; but he does nothing of all this that is in his power, but pleases himself with what he would do if his power was greater.

Come to thy senses, Clemens. Make the best use of thy present state. Do now as thou thinkest thou would do with a great estate. Be sparing, deny thyself, abstain from all vanities, that the poor may be better maintained, and then thou art as charitable as thou canst be in any estate.

—William Law

WHEN YOU'RE TIRED, WEIGHED DOWN WITH PERSONAL MATTERS OR LOOMING DEADLINES, THAT'S WHEN BEING KIND TO OTHERS IS THE HARDEST. IT'S ALSO THE TIME IT LOOKS BEST ON YOU.

SAMUEL
LIFELONG OBEDIENCE

SELECTIONS FROM 1 SAMUEL 12

After a life spent in the spotlight, leading Israel through the difficult transition from the judges to kingly rule, Samuel presented himself to the people one last time— to right any wrongs, to make any amends. But the books were clear. He had been faithful for the long haul.

Samuel said to all Israel . . . "As for me, I'm old and gray. . . . I've led you from my youth until this day. Here I am. Bring charges against me before the LORD and His anointed. Whose ox have I taken? Whose donkey have I taken? Whom have I wronged? Whom have I mistreated? From whose hand have I taken a bribe to look the other way? I will make it right with you."

"You haven't wronged us; you haven't mistreated us; and you haven't taken anything from anyone's hand," they responded.

So he said to them, "The LORD is a witness against you, and His anointed is a witness today that you haven't found anything in my hand."

Samuel is one of a handful of Bible personalities we get to know from birth to death. We first meet him as a child in the Lord's house at Shiloh, learning to listen to God's voice. We see him painfully passing the baton to a weak-kneed wanna-be named Saul. We watch him giving his blessing to a shepherd boy with the heart of a king. In fact, we even catch a glimpse of him beyond the grave, conjured up by the witch of Endor. Yet from start to finish, from beginning to end, we find him one hundred percent faithful.

LOOK AT IT THIS WAY

One thing I would earnestly recommend to you who are afraid of backsliding and apostasy: Say to yourself: "Whether I get to Canaan or not, I will never go back to Egypt. I will die with my face toward God and holiness. Lord God, if I am cast away, if you never give me joy again, yet I will never cease to look to your mercy in Christ Jesus, for there only have I hope. By your grace I will die with my face to the cross."

Did you ever hear of anybody who perished in that position? No. It shall never be reported in heaven above or in hell beneath that a soul died that way. No soul can perish whose eyes look toward the five wounds of Jesus crucified. He is the way, the living way, the only way, the sure way: Follow him.

Do as the blind man did who followed Jesus in the way: rise up now, for he calls you. Look to Jesus! Take this road of refuge, this way of grace. May God the Holy Spirit help you to take to the way at once, without delay!

–Charles Spurgeon

THE DEMANDS OF PERSONAL RIGHTEOUSNESS SOMETIMES SEEM SO HARD— *TOO* HARD. BUT IMAGINE BEING ABLE TO LOOK BACK LATER WITH NO REGRETS. DOESN'T THAT SOUND WORTH IT ALL?

SAUL
A LOSER AT LEADERSHIP

SELECTIONS FROM 1 SAMUEL 15

Saul has to go down in history as the biggest opportunity waster in all the Bible. Tall, handsome, brimming with potential, chosen by the Lord as Israel's very first king, filled full with the Spirit of God. The stuff of legends was his to write. But legends don't lack leadership.

Early in the morning Samuel got up to confront Saul, but it was reported to Samuel, "Saul went to Carmel where he set up a monument for himself.". . . When Samuel came to Saul, Saul said, "Blessed are you of the Lord. I've carried out the LORD's instructions." Samuel retorted, "Then what's this sound of sheep in my ears and the sound of cattle that I'm hearing?". . .

Saul responded to Samuel, "But I did obey the LORD! . . . The troops took sheep and cattle from the plunder—the best of what was set apart for destruction—to sacrifice to the LORD your God at Gilgal." Then Samuel said, "Does the LORD take pleasure in burnt offerings and sacrifices as much as in obeying the LORD?"

When you compare the sins of Saul with those of David, a confusing equation develops. David, as you know, didn't stop at adultery but turned his mistake into murder. Those are two biggies. All Saul really did to warrant God's anger was to offer a sacrifice out of turn and to bring an enemy king back alive when he had been ordered killed. Minor violations? On the surface, maybe. But David melted before his accuser in sorrow and repentance. Saul met his accuser with excuses. His true colors were already starting to show.

LOOK AT IT THIS WAY

Great numbers of us, in all walks of life, do not live our lives in line with traditional standards for ethical conduct. Too many of us have embraced the modern-day, conditional approach to integrity. As a result, we too often capitulate to the virus of dishonesty and lower our standards for conduct. We too often take wrong action when the pressure is on in order to gain a false sense of personal advantage.

Moral immaturity is motivated by personal profit, prestige, or pleasure instead of an intentional decision to do what's right. Compromising our character occurs when we underestimate evil and flirt with temptations of all kinds. Compromising our character is always just a choice away; it is enticed through flattery and fantasy. It ensnares us and brings about dishonest rationalizations and deceptions when we refuse to think about the rightness of our actions.

It is time for us to intentionally focus on God's proven values and principles for living and working. Then we will gain the maximum benefits of a balanced life and make this world a better place to live.

—Millard MacAdam

> SAUL'S BIGGEST PROBLEM WAS NOT BEING ABLE TO ADMIT HE WAS WRONG. ALWAYS BE WILLING TO FACE UP TO YOUR MISTAKES, AND NEVER THINK YOUR WAY IS THE ONLY ONE.

JONATHAN
A FRIEND TO THE END

Jonathan and David had practically grown up together. Inseparable. But the years can change a friendship. And if Jonathan shared even a little of his father Saul's contempt, could David still trust him? Yes. Something in Jonathan's eyes made it clear. He was a friend for life.

Saul ordered his son Jonathan and all his servants to kill David. Saul's son Jonathan, however, liked David very much, so he told David: "My father Saul is seeking to kill you. So you should be on your guard in the morning. Stay in a secret place and hide yourself.. . .

In the morning Jonathan went out to the field for the appointed meeting with David. . . . He and Jonathan kissed each other and wept with each other, though David wept the hardest.

Jonathan said to David, "Go in the peace the two of us pledged in the name of the LORD when we said, 'The LORD will be a witness between you and me and between my offspring and your offspring forever.' "

Friends are an important part of who we are. But the demands of marriage and family change the playing field of friendship, severing some of the spontaneity of single life. That's why it's so important for husbands and wives to become friends—genuinely enjoying each other's company, looking for ways to be thoughtful, standing as a united front against the foes that threaten their commitment to each other, their family, their God. If you'll make your relationship top priority, the best friend you'll ever have is the one you married.

LOOK AT IT THIS WAY

Not everyone is as blessed as these two men in connecting with a friend for life. I believe it is something most desire, but many—especially men—find it hard to attain. Madison Avenue realizes and acknowledges this. Just think about the way they choose to market products, such as beer. Beer commercials are directed (not so subtly) at men, and they promise two things: beautiful women and meaningful friendships with other guys who share a common gusto for life. The reason these guy-commercials are so designed is because the advertising agencies know men are looking for these kinds of relationships, but very few have them.

Perhaps Jonathan had looked all over Israel for a man who matched him in heart and mind. Perhaps he was as frustrated as some today because of his lack of meaningful friendships. But even though he was on the opposite end of the socioeconomic spectrum, as soon as he saw David, he instantly reached out in friendship—a relationship which became one of the most consistent and defining aspects of their lives.

—Jim Henry

THE GROUND RULES OF FRIENDSHIP HAVEN'T REALLY CHANGED MUCH SINCE WE WERE KIDS. TO HAVE A FRIEND, BE A FRIEND—THE KIND OF FRIEND OTHERS CAN COUNT ON. THEN YOU'LL HAVE A TREASURE FOR LIFE.

DAVID
BIGGER THAN BETRAYAL

SELECTIONS FROM 1 SAMUEL 24

If anybody had good reason for putting a knife in Saul's back, it was David. But when David looked at Saul, he didn't see a man intent on killing him, didn't remember the spear coming straight for his neck. He saw the chosen of God. And that's all that mattered.

Saul took 3,000 of Israel's choice men and went to look for David. . . . When Saul came to the sheep pens along the road, there was a cave there, and he went in to relieve himself. . . . Then David went up and secretly cut off the corner of Saul's robe. . . .

Saul left the cave and went on his way. After that, David got up, went out of the cave, and called to Saul, "My lord the king! . . . Why do you listen to the words of people who say 'Look! David intends to harm you'? This very day you can see with your own eyes that the Lord handed you over to me in the cave. Someone advised me to kill you, but I took pity on you and said, 'I won't raise my hand against my lord, for he is the Lord's anointed.

David's godly restraint is reminiscent of another who would endure the blows of injustice, who would walk beneath his heavenly calling for a season in order to be obedient to God and submissive to his timetable. The blood of David's royal line would one day soak a dirty hillside outside Jerusalem, pulsating from the hands, head, and feet of one with an unbending respect for God's authority. Like David, no one could have faulted Jesus for taking the path of revenge. But only God's way brings a true reward.

LOOK AT IT THIS WAY

Though David followed God's principles in dealing with Saul, he realized he could never fully trust the king again. This is apparent from David's behavior—and understandably so. When Saul invited David to come and be in his presence following the second encounter, David's reply was kind but negative. He had made his point with Saul—he did not return evil for evil—but he could not entrust his life to the king.

As Christians, we must forgive one another. I believe we are also to do everything we can to reestablish trust, even going the extra mile in reaching out to our enemies. However, there are times when it is no longer possible to trust another person totally. Like Saul, some people demonstrate again and again their untrustworthiness and unpredictable behavior.

David was saying he would never take Saul's life. However, he also was saying that the only one who could ultimately protect his life from Saul was the Lord. Never again would he trust the king.

—*Gene Getz*

DAVID
UNINHIBITED WORSHIP

SELECTIONS FROM 2 SAMUEL 6

Like all of us, David had trouble with some things in his life. But worship wasn't one of them. Pain couldn't stifle or suppress it. Pleasure couldn't surpass it. In worship everything else took a distant second to pouring his heart, soul, and mind into exalting the name of his God.

David, wearing a linen ephod, was dancing with all his might before the LORD. He and the whole house of Israel were bringing up the ark of the LORD with shouts and the sound of the ram's horn. . . . When David returned home to bless his household, Saul's daughter Michal came out to meet him. "How the king of Israel honored himself today!" she said. "He revealed himself today in the sight of his servants' maids just like one of the worthless people would reveal himself!"

David replied to Michal . . . "I'll continue to celebrate before the LORD, and I'll demean myself more than this and consider myself lowly."

Just a guess: When you hear the words *uninhibited worship,* you probably think of people swinging from the chandeliers, dancing in the aisles, jumping like jackrabbits in some kind of frenzied rejoicing. Maybe we all could use a taste of that from time to time, but that's not what uninhibited worship is at all. It can happen in the quietest of places, in the simplest of ways, when we lose all the worries about form and formality, when our love for God saturates our spirit—till worship ceases to be a drill and becomes a delight.

LOOK AT IT THIS WAY

When I stepped into the small, inviting chapel, I also stepped into my first experience with the liturgical. I wasn't accustomed to the worship environment—to the large table balancing the pulpit, to burning candles, to a worship leader dressed in vestments, to a guitar and folk songs mixed with an ancient chant and a classic hymn. I wasn't familiar with the kind of participation demanded of me—the dialogue, acclamation, and three Scripture readings punctuated by psalms, the bidding prayers, the passing of the peace, the personal touch of the priest calling me by name as he gave me the bread and wine, and the praise and celebration expressed in the Communion song.

You might say I was surprised by joy! I found myself ministering to God in praise, and God in turn was ministering to me. A new worship experience had bumped up against an old prejudice of mine, and a new attitude was born. I had taken into myself the experience of another tradition, I had been in dialogue with another worship tradition, and I was surely the richer for it.

—Robert Webber

DO IT RIGHT NOW. RIGHT WHERE YOU ARE. BEGIN PRAISING GOD. OUT LOUD OR IN SILENCE, TILL NOTHING ELSE MATTERS. WE'LL BE DOING IT FOREVER. NOW'S A GREAT TIME TO START LOVING IT.

DAVID
COMMITTED TO COMPASSION

SELECTIONS FROM 2 SAMUEL 9

King David, weary from constant demands on his time, finally gets a few minutes to himself. He sits down, takes a deep breath, and starts to think. About going to the beach? Winning his next battle? Would you believe inviting a poor cripple to come live in the palace?

David inquired, "Is there anyone remaining from Saul's family to whom I may show kindness for Jonathan's sake?"...

"There is still Jonathan's son who is crippled in both feet," Ziba replied to the king. . . . So King David had him brought from the house of Machir son of Ammiel in Lo-debar. Mephibosheth son of Jonathan son of Saul came to David, bowed his face toward the ground, and prostrated himself. . . . "Don't be afraid," David said to him, "because I intend to show you kindness for the sake of your father Jonathan: I will restore to you all your grandfather Saul's fields, and you will always eat meals at my table.". . . So Mephibosheth ate at David's table just like one of the king's sons.

Compassion is the quickest way to the heart of God. It's written all over the Bible, confirmed throughout ages of history, and verified by the deep feeling of rightness that caresses your spirit when you show kindness to someone who needs your help. But it costs you. Maybe a lazy Sunday afternoon. Maybe a meal. Maybe a few hours of sleep. But it earns you a lot more than you give up. Hugs. Laughter. Joy. And a hunger to give even more, to care even more deeply, to be more like Christ, to love others with compassion.

LOOK AT IT THIS WAY

There is ingrained in the depths of human nature a dislike of the general ruck of mankind, in spite of all our modern jargon about loving humanity. We have a disparaging way of talking about the common crowd; though the common crowd is made up of innumerable editions of you and me.

Ask the Holy Spirit to enable your mind to brood for one moment on the value of the "nobody" to Jesus. The people who make up the common crowd are nobodies to me, but it is astonishing to find that it is the nobodies that Jesus Christ came to save.

The terms we use for men in the sense of their social position are nothing to him. There is no room in Christianity, as Jesus Christ taught it, for philanthropic or social patronage. Jesus Christ never patronized anyone. He came straight down to where men live in order that the supreme gift he came to give might be theirs. It is only by getting our minds into the state of the mind of Jesus that we can understand how it is possible to fulfill the royal law and love our neighbor as ourselves.

—Oswald Chambers

THINK OF SOMETHING SACRIFICIAL YOU CAN DO THIS WEEK, A WAY TO SHOW COMPASSION TO SOMEONE WHO CAN'T PAY YOU BACK, JUST FOR THE JOY OF IT. IT'S ONE OF THE PUREST ACTS OF WORSHIP.

DAVID
READY TO REPENT

SELECTIONS FROM PSALMS 32 & 51

David never thought this day would come. He never would have believed he could fall so far, stoop so low. The prophet Nathan's words burned like an acid bath. "You are the man!" Rocked on his heels, hands to his chest, the real David returned. In repentance.

When I kept silent, my bones became brittle from my groaning all day long. For day and night Your hand was heavy on me; my strength was drained as in the summer's heat. Then I acknowledged my sin to You and did not conceal my iniquity. I said, "I will confess my transgressions to the LORD," and You took away the guilt of my sin. . . .

Purify me with hyssop, and I will be clean; wash me, and I will be whiter than snow. Let me hear joy and gladness; let the bones You have crushed rejoice. . . . Create a clean heart for me and renew a steadfast spirit within me. . . . God, You will not despise a broken and humbled heart.

There is confession. There is repentance. And there is a difference. David confessed. He admitted his mistake. That's half the battle. But repentance is the tough part. Confession finishes its work in a moment. Repentance takes a lifetime. Repentance means facing the same temptation again. And again. And again. And again. And saying no every time. And when you slip and say yes, it means getting back up—and saying no again. It's a painful path, a bruising battle, but every other road is a lie. Repentance is the only way home.

LOOK AT IT THIS WAY

Sometimes, alas, sin even prevails over us, and we are forced in deep anguish to confess that we have fallen beneath its power. Who among us can say, "I am clean, I have not sinned"? Still, a temporary defeat is not sufficient to effect a total subjugation. Sin shall not have dominion over the believer, for though he falls, he shall rise again.

The child of God when he falls into the mire is like the sheep that gets up and escapes from the ditch as quickly as possible; it is not his nature to lie there. The ungodly man is like the hog that rolls in the filth and wallows in it with delight. The mire has dominion over the swine, but it has none over the sheep. With many bleatings and outcries, the sheep seeks the shepherd again, but not so the swine. Every child of God weeps, mourns, and bemoans his sin, and he hates it when for a while he has been overtaken by it. Sin has an awful power, but it has no dominion; it casts us down, but it cannot make us take delight in its evil.

—Charles Spurgeon

REPENT OF IT TODAY. THAT SIN. YOU KNOW THE ONE. THAT ONE THAT OVERTAKES YOU NO MATTER HOW FAST YOU RUN. SATAN WILL LAUGH AND SAY YOU CAN'T BE TRUSTED. AND YOU KNOW HE'S RIGHT. BUT GOD CAN.

DAVID
ACCEPTING DISAPPOINTMENT

SELECTIONS FROM 1 CHRONICLES 17

No one loved to worship more than David did. Of the three kings who ruled over an undivided Israel, David stood head and shoulders above them all. If anyone deserved to oversee the building of the first temple, it was David. But it wasn't to be. And he took it like a man.

The word of God came to Nathan: "Go to David My servant and say, 'This is what the LORD says: You are not the one to build Me a house to dwell in. . . . When your time comes to go be with your fathers, I will raise up after you your descendant, who is one of your own sons, and I will establish his kingdom. He will build a house for Me, and I will establish his throne forever. . . .'"

King David went in, sat in the LORD's presence, and said, "Who am I, LORD God, and what is my house, that You have brought me this far? . . . Let the word that You have spoken concerning Your servant and his house be confirmed forever, and do as You have spoken. Let Your name be confirmed and magnified forever."

Life's not fair. We've all said it or thought it. We've all wished it weren't true. But it is. Life's not fair. Sorry. But as believers in Jesus Christ, can't we all equally attest that our reward isn't fair either? Hope? Heaven? Forgiveness? Righteousness? Member in good standing in the glorious, eternal kingdom of God? To say we deserve far less is to not say it convincingly enough. Of all the unfair things in life, God's approving nod of grace toward us is the most unwarranted act of all. Hallelujah! Life's not fair!

LOOK AT IT THIS WAY

Do you have some cherished desire that you know you are going to have to relinquish? As we get older, many of us see that some of those great hopes and dreams are never going to be realized. Perhaps it is a dream of some great accomplishment through a unique kind of ministry. Maybe it is a desire for a certain kind of career or recognition. Maybe it is a desire for romance and marriage. Maybe it's a hope for relief from something in your life that you've had to live with for years. Whatever it is, you may now recognize that it is never going to happen, and that's a hard pill to swallow. But, like David, it's an opportunity to find satisfaction in what God has allowed you to do.

We can live the last years of our life swamped by guilt or overwhelmed by failures of the past. Or we can say, "By the grace of God, I did the best I could with what I had. And I claim his promise that somehow he'll use what I did accomplish for his greater glory."

—Charles Swindoll

HAVE YOU HAD TO FACE DISAPPOINTMENT LATELY? IN YOUR JOB, YOUR RELATIONSHIPS, YOUR HEALTH? NO MATTER HOW DOWN YOU FEEL, GOD CAN GET DOWN BENEATH YOU. AND HE WILL KEEP YOU UP.

DAVID
PASSING DOWN A BLESSING

SELECTIONS FROM 1 CHRONICLES 22 & 28

As quick on the trigger as David was, you just know that in his final words to Solomon, he had to search hard for breath between sniffles and sobs. But the pride was coming the other way, too— from a son who had seen these words lived, who had seen a good picture of God in his dad.

"Now, my son, may the Lord be with you. . . . Above all, may the Lord give you insight and understanding when He puts you in charge of Israel so that you may keep the law of the Lord your God. Then you will be succeed if you carefully follow the statutes and ordinances that the Lord commanded Moses for Israel. Be strong and courageous. Don't be afraid or dismayed. . . .

"Solomon my son, know the God of your father, and serve Him with a whole heart and a willing mind, for the Lord searches every heart and understands the intention of every thought. If you seek Him, He will be found by you, but if you forsake Him, He will reject you forever."

Blessings between parent and child don't have to be confined to the tearful drama of the deathbed. They can happen as you go, in the most casual of circumstances. In enthusiastic cheers from the bleachers. In words of forgiveness spoken to the top of their shame-heavy heads. In time carved out of your busy schedule especially for them. In a phone call out of the blue or a handwritten letter with a batch of your wife's homemade brownies. Blessings can be shared just about anywhere, appreciated just about anytime.

LOOK AT IT THIS WAY

When it comes to pictures about their future, children are literalists. For this reason, communicating a special future to a child is so important. When a person feels in his heart that the future is hopeful and something to look forward to, it can greatly affect his attitude on life. In this way, we are providing our children a clear light for their path in life.

Children begin to take steps down the positive pathway pictured for them when they hear words like these: "God has given you such a sensitive heart. I wouldn't be surprised if you end up helping a great many people when you grow older," or "You are such a good helper. When you grow up and marry someday, you're going to be such a help to your wife (or husband) and family."

We as parents cannot predict our children's future with biblical accuracy, but we can provide them with the hope and direction that is part of picturing meaningful goals. Our children can begin to live up to these goals and so will gain added security in an insecure world.

—Gary Smalley and John Trent

MAKE TIME TO TELL YOUR CHILDREN HOW PROUD YOU ARE OF THEM, TO SHARE A VERSE THAT STRUCK YOU IN YOUR QUIET TIME, TO LET THEM KNOW THEY'VE BEEN ON YOUR MIND. IT'LL BLESS THEIR HEARTS.

DAVID
GIVEN TO GOOD STEWARDSHIP

SELECTIONS FROM 1 CHRONICLES 29

David closes his life preparing for something he'll never get to see—Israel's great house of worship, the temple he so longed to build. But even impending death couldn't dim his excitement for giving. He knew at seventy-one years old what he'd known all his life. Everything is God's.

The people rejoiced because of their leaders' willingness to give, for they had given to the LORD with a whole heart. King David also rejoiced greatly. Then David praised the LORD in the sight of all the assembly. . . .

"O LORD our God, all this wealth that we've provided for building You a house for Your holy name comes from Your hand; everything belongs to You. . . . I've willingly given all these things with an upright heart, and now I've seen Your people who are present here giving joyfully and willingly to You. O LORD God of Abraham, Isaac, and Israel, our forefathers, keep this intention forever in the thoughts of the hearts of Your people, and confirm their hearts toward You."

David possessed the visionary qualities of all great leaders: the ability to invest in things bigger than himself, the drive to pursue goals and dreams laid up in store for future generations. But putting that principle to work requires a sound perspective on godly stewardship. Before we can lose ourselves in the big picture, we must first be willing to paint ourselves out of it, to loosen our controlling grip on people and things, to watch God perform his work with the resources he's given. It's his ball, his game, his field. Go, God, go.

LOOK AT IT THIS WAY

We don't own anything. God owns everything, and we are his managers. For most of us, the house we now call "my house" was called "my house" by someone else a few years ago. And a few years from now, someone else will call that house "my house." Do you own any land? A few years from now, someone else will be calling it "my land." We are just temporary stewards of things that belong to God. You probably believe that in theory already, but your giving will be a reflection of how much you genuinely believe it.

God has specifically said that he owns not just the things we possess, but even the money under our name in the bank and the currency in our wallets. So the question is not, *How much of my money should I give to God?* but rather, *How much of God's money should I keep for myself?*

When we put a check or cash in the offering plate, we should give it with the belief that all we have belongs to God and with the commitment that we will use all of it as he wants.

—Donald Whitney

IT'S NOT EASY TO GIVE . . . UNTIL YOU START. SO WHAT ARE YOU WAITING FOR? IF YOU WANT BLESSINGS YOU'LL NEVER BE ABLE TO CONTAIN, JOIN THE JOYFUL ARMY OF THE GENEROUS.

SOLOMON
CHOOSING WISDOM

SELECTIONS FROM 1 KINGS 3

It was the first time he had pondered this question in a dream state, maybe, but he'd done it many times before in his right mind. How in the world could he live up to the job of king? How could he follow an act like his father David? This was too big for one man.

At Gibeon the LORD appeared to Solomon in a dream at night; God said, "Ask! What should I give you?"...

"O LORD my God, You have made Your servant king in my father David's place. Yet I am but a little boy; I don't know how to go out or come in. Your servant is among Your people whom You have chosen, a numerous people, too numerous to be numbered or counted. So give Your servant an obedient heart to judge Your people, discerning between good and evil. For who can judge this magnificent people of Yours?"

It pleased the LORD that Solomon had requested this.

Knowledge is a microwave, serving up quick bits of information in five-minute bursts of news, traffic, and weather. It's a fast-food overload of the trivial and temporary, filling our head with chunks of processed facts. But pursuing wisdom is like cooking with a crock pot. It doesn't pop and sizzle. It doesn't glow red hot. And it won't be ready in ten minutes, even on its highest setting. But when the time is right, when all the spices and flavorings and juices have soaked through, you'll have something that's really worth sharing.

LOOK AT IT THIS WAY

The Hebrew word for wisdom refers to much more than an accumulation of facts. In the Old Testament, this word was used for anyone who had an unusual degree of skill in a given area. For instance, if a potter could create beautiful tableware, he was said to have wisdom. The word means to be skilled in some area of life. In biblical terms wisdom might be defined as the ability to live life skillfully from God's point of view. It comes from viewing life from a vertical perspective and acting accordingly.

But let no man think he will become wise by accident. No, a man must search after wisdom as if he were searching for silver or gold; he must set aside trivial pursuits in favor of that which comes only from God. You must turn from evil if you really want wisdom. But there is a further step you must take. It involves humbling yourself, admitting your need, confessing your lack, and asking God to help you. If you want wisdom, you can have it. It's free, but it will cost all you have.

—Ray Pritchard

WISDOM TAKES TIME, MOMENTS OF QUIET REFLECTION AND THOUGHTFUL OBSERVATION, AND AN OPEN EAR TO GOD IN PRAYER AND BIBLE STUDY. IT WON'T HAPPEN OVERNIGHT, BUT IT WILL LAST OVER TIME.

SOLOMON
TURNING AWAY

SELECTIONS FROM 1 KINGS 11

As it turned out, the wise man played the fool. Solomon found more to love in the treasures and pleasures of the world than he did in God. And yet for all his wealth and all his women, he left behind a legacy of bitterness and emptiness. Hope it was worth it.

In addition to Pharaoh's daughter, King Solomon loved many foreign women: Moabite, Ammonite, Edomite, Sidonian and Hittite women from the nations about which the LORD had said to the Israelites, "You must not intermingle with them, and they must not intermingle with you; they are certain to turn your hearts to follow their own gods." It was these Solomon clung to in love. . . .

During Solomon's old age his wives turned his heart toward other gods. His heart was not wholly with the LORD his God, as his father David's heart had been. . . . So Solomon did what was evil in the LORD's eyes, and unlike his father David, he did not completely follow the LORD.

Solomon's slippery slope into self-destruction says a lot about the weight of our choices. For not only did his lust for life's delicacies cost him the favor of God and a lasting legacy of godliness, but it set in motion the entire collapse of the known Israelite world. That's because choices never exist in a vacuum. And their consequences—whether for good or evil—compound over time. Each of us stands on the shoulders of choices made not only by us but also by others. It pays to make good ones, no matter how small.

LOOK AT IT THIS WAY

Christ said it was difficult for "the rich" to enter the kingdom of heaven, referring, no doubt, to "riches" in the ordinary sense. But I think it really covers riches in every sense—good fortune, health, popularity, and all the things one wants to have. All these things tend—just as money tends—to make you feel independent of God, because if you have them you are happy and already contented in this life. You don't want to turn away to anything more, and so you try to rest in a shadowy happiness as if it could last forever.

But God wants to give you a real and eternal happiness. Consequently he may have to take all these "riches" away from you; if he doesn't, you will go on relying on them. It sounds cruel, doesn't it? But I am beginning to find out that what people call the "cruel" doctrines are really the kindest in the long run. If you think of this world as a place intended simply for our happiness, you find it quite intolerable; think of it as a place of training and correction and it is not so bad.

—*C. S. Lewis*

THE THOUGHT OF TURNING AWAY BECOMES MORE DISTANT THE CLOSER YOU GET TO CHRIST. REMIND YOURSELF OFTEN THAT YOU'RE IN HIS PRESENCE. REMEMBER THAT HE DIDN'T QUIT ON YOU.

REHOBOAM
IN BAD COMPANY

SELECTIONS FROM 1 KINGS 12

Old men for wisdom, young men for war. It's an adage as timeless as it is true, and those who trample on it get to learn their lessons the hard way. Solomon's son, Rehoboam—like those in each generation—got his chance to accept or reject it. He paid a youthful price.

Jeroboam and all the assembly of Israel came and spoke with Rehoboam: "Your father made our yoke harsh. You, therefore, lighten your father's harsh service and the heavy yoke he put on us, and we will serve you.". . .

Then King Rehoboam consulted with the elders who had served his father Solomon. . . . They replied, "If today you will be a servant to this people and serve them, and if you respond to them by speaking kind words to them, then they'll be your servants forever." But he rejected the advice of the elders who had advised him, and he consulted with the young men who had grown up with him and served him.

Our gut tells us we should associate freely with anyone, not to discriminate by holiness ratings. And that's basically true, as far as being an in-the-world-not-of-the-world example of Christ's love and grace. But the Bible's pretty clear about the distance we should keep from those who don't share our belief system. "Come out from among them and be separate" (2 Corinthians 6:17). "Avoid these people!" (2 Timothy 3:5b). Yes, serve everyone. Love everyone. But when it comes to close friendships, guard your perimeter.

LOOK AT IT THIS WAY

Days should speak.

It was an instance of Rehoboam's weakness that he did not prefer aged counselors, but had a better opinion of the young men that had grown up with him and with whom he was familiar. It was a folly for him to think that, because they had been his agreeable companions in the sports and pleasures of his youth, they were therefore fit to have the management of the affairs of his kingdom. Great wits have not always the most wisdom; nor are those to be relied on as our best friends that know how to make us merry, for that will not make us happy.

It is of great consequence to young people, that are setting out in the world, whom they associate with, accommodate themselves to, and depend upon for advice. If they reckon those their best friends that feed their pride, gratify their vanity, and further them in their pleasures, they are already marked for ruin. No more needs to be done to ruin men than to leave them to themselves and their own pride and passion.

—Matthew Henry

ADVICE COMES FROM ALL DIRECTIONS, IN MANY DIFFERENT FORMS, ON LOTS OF DIFFERENT SUBJECTS. MAKE SURE YOU HAVE PEOPLE AROUND YOU WHOSE ADVICE YOU CAN TRUST. THEY'RE WORTH SEEKING OUT.

ASA
CONFRONTING FAMILY

SELECTIONS FROM 2 CHRONICLES 14 & 15

Busting up altars to pagan gods and smashing the tools of their trickery was one of King Asa's most rewarding pursuits. He knew his cause was right, and he was ready to answer anyone who thought he was taking his religious purity too far. But what if the goddess worshiper was Grandma?

Asa did what was good and right in the eyes of the LORD his God. He removed the pagan altars and the high places. He shattered their sacred pillars and chopped down their Asherah poles. He told the people of Judah to seek the LORD God of their fathers and to carry out the law and the commandment. He also removed from all the cities of Judah the high places and the incense altars, and the kingdom experienced peace under him. . . .

Asa also removed Maacah, King Asa's grandmother, from being queen mother because she had made a horrid image of Asherah. Asa chopped down her horrid image then crushed it and burned it in the Wadi Kidron.

Something takes over when we get around our families. We turn into kids again. We become not who we are but who they see us to be. And to a degree, that's fine. It's wonderful to recapture a sense of the past, to retrace our steps with those who remember. But intensive care waiting rooms are coming. Late night phone calls are coming. Funeral homes are coming. And we'll wish we'd been mature enough to let God shine through our conversation. We'll wish we hadn't been so hesitant to share what's really important to us.

LOOK AT IT THIS WAY

One of the biggest reasons why most Christians tremble at the thought of witnessing to their own families is that those are the people who know them so well. They can smell the slightest hint of baloney on their breath. But your family's need of Christ has nothing to do with what you have to offer, other than your total honesty about his grace and goodness toward you. What you want to show them is his worth. And the way to do that is to be truthful about his work in you, about your struggles as well as your successes.

You'll be a much more effective Christian just letting your loved ones see that you're still yourself or, more accurately, that you're *finally* yourself. Let them watch you in process, as you submit to the Holy Spirit's work in your life. Let them be inspired by a true artist at work, as he chisels away the stony facade of all that inherited sin and reveals the real, redeemable you.

They still won't see a perfect person. But you can let them see God's perfect work as he performs it in you.

—*Jim Gilbert*

YOU'RE NOT CALLED TO BE THE JUDGE OF YOUR FAMILY'S FAITH. BUT YOU ARE CALLED TO DEMONSTRATE CHRIST'S LOVE TO THEM AND TO STAND UP FOR HIS NAME EVEN WHEN IT'S UNACCEPTABLE.

AHAB
RECOGNIZING GOD'S POWER

SELECTIONS FROM 1 KINGS 21

Ahab was a scoundrel. No two ways about it. He and his wicked wife, Jezebel, thumbed their nose at God their whole life and made a mockery of Israel's throne. But there was a day when God got Ahab's attention— the day Ahab realized he wasn't the only king in town.

The word of the LORD came to Elijah the Tishbite: "Get up; go down to meet Ahab king of Israel, who is in Samaria. You'll find him in Naboth's vineyard, where he has gone down to take possession of it. Tell him . . . 'In the place where the dogs licked Naboth's blood, the dogs will lick your blood—yes, yours!' " . . .

When Ahab heard these words, he tore his clothes, put sackcloth over his body, and fasted. He lay down in sackcloth and walked about subdued. Then the word of the LORD came to Elijah the Tishbite: "Have you seen how Ahab has humbled himself before me? Because he has humbled himself before me I will not bring the disaster during his lifetime."

God was gracious to Ahab, but don't interpret the king's actions as much more than fleeting humility. He died a coward on the battlefield, still resisting the word of the Lord. Ahab's melancholy merely proves that there are two kinds of sorrow a person can have over sin: godly sorrow and worldly sorrow (2 Corinthians 7:10). One produces repentance; the other produces death. For a moment Ahab felt sick enough to change his diet of deceit and debauchery. But that was before he dismissed it as just a bad case of heartburn.

LOOK AT IT THIS WAY

Long ago, England was ruled by a king named Canute. Like many leaders and men of power, Canute was surrounded by people who were always praising him. Every time he walked into a room, the flattery began. "So you say I am the greatest man in the world?" he asked them. "In that case, bring me my chair, and we will go down to the water." The men scurried to carry his chair over the sands.

"Sea!" cried Canute, "I command you to come no further! Waves, stop your rolling! Surf, stop your pounding! Do not dare touch my feet!"

The tide came in, just as it always did. It came up around the king's chair, wetting not only his feet, but also his robe. "Well, my friends," Canute said, "it seems I do not have quite so much power as you would have me believe. Perhaps now you will remember there is only one King who is all-powerful, and it is he who rules the sea and holds the ocean in the hollow of his hand. I suggest you reserve your praises for him."

And some say Canute took off his crown soon afterward and never wore it again.

—*James Baldwin*

BEGIN EACH DAY REMINDING YOURSELF WHO'S IN CHARGE OF YOUR LIFE. IT'S ALWAYS EASIER TO ASCRIBE POWER TO HIM RATHER THAN HAVING IT PROVEN TO YOU AGAINST YOUR WILL.

ELIJAH
DEALING WITH DISCOURAGEMENT

SELECTIONS FROM 1 KINGS 19

He was a rugged, woodsy, mountain man— a fiery Old Testament version of John the Baptist. But even a tough nut like Elijah could crack under the pressure of public opinion and the paralyzing fear of death threats. It was enough to make a guy question everything.

Ahab told Jezebel everything that Elijah had done and how he had killed all the prophets with the sword. So Jezebel sent a messenger to Elijah, saying, "May the gods punish me and do so severely if by this time tomorrow I don't make your life like the life of one of them!" Then he became afraid and immediately fled for his life. . . .

The word of the LORD came to him, and He said to him, "What are you doing here, Elijah?"

"I have been very zealous for the LORD God of Hosts," he replied, "but the Israelites have forsaken Your covenant, torn down Your altars, and killed Your prophets with the sword. I alone am left, and they're looking for me in order to take my life."

There's always a remnant—people who aren't willing to blend into the world's fabric but are cut from a different cloth. They may never be recognized for their outstanding achievements. They just quietly, patiently, persistently, prayerfully put their trust in God—even when no one's looking. Elijah hadn't seen them—seven thousand invisible people scattered along the streets, hillsides, and backwaters of Israel, whispering prayers of praise to God. It's a wonder he hadn't noticed them, but not when all he could see were his own problems.

Drained People ... made fools of themselves
usefulness is over

LOOK AT IT THIS WAY

Individuals in a drained condition feel caught up in a sea of feelings that often runs counter to all the facts. There are strong senses of self-doubt and negativism. The mind seeks out all the possible errors that might have been made in the past hours, and then it amplifies them until all positive contributions are mentally blocked out. Drained people become supercritical of self and of others. They are convinced they have made fools of themselves.

When men and women are drained, they often generate moods that lead to their wanting to quit the tasks they've wanted to do the most. Like Elijah, they are convinced that their usefulness is over, that they are powerless to go any further.

The Boston Marathon runner at Heartbreak Hill in Newton isn't surprised. He knows from experience and from the descriptions of others that he will feel exhausted and ready to quit as he plods along. And he doesn't quit because he knows what weariness is all about and where it comes from. The passion to finish the course and to win remains.

—Gordon MacDonald

IT'S NATURAL TO FEEL DIS-ILLUSIONED AT TIMES—WHEN PEOPLE DIS-APPOINT YOU, WHEN TROUBLES PILE UP. BUT GOD CAN GIVE YOU SUPER-NATURAL FAITH TO SURVIVE. DON'T WORRY. YOU'RE NOT ALONE.

ELIJAH
TRUTH IN HIGH PLACES

SELECTIONS FROM 2 KINGS 1: 2-3

It's one thing to express your indignant political opinions over dinner conversation. It's another to look straight into the eye of a world leader who could call for your head at the snap of his fingers and specifically outline his downfall. It takes more than guts, actually. It takes God.

Ahaziah fell through the lattice of his upper chamber in Samaria and was injured. Therefore he sent messengers and said to them, "Go. Inquire of Baal-zebub the god of Ekron whether I will recover from this injury."

But the angel of the LORD spoke to Elijah the Tishbite, "Get up. Go up to meet the messengers of the king of Samaria, and speak to them, 'Is it because there is no God in Israel that you are going to inquire of Baal-zebub the god of Ekron?' Now, therefore, thus says the LORD, 'You shall not get up from your sickbed, for you will most certainly die.'

Ahaziah wasn't the only Israelite king to feel the heat of Elijah's indignation. The granddaddy of them all was Ahab, whose penchant for cultivating economic ties with neighboring nations had softened Israel's royal tolerance for pagan worship. Nothing got Elijah's dander up quicker than that. So in his generation he was the conscience of Israel, and his faithfulness to stand up against blasphemy and injustice at the highest levels is a reminder that each of us has a responsibility to hold our leaders accountable for their actions.

LOOK AT IT THIS WAY

Great Commission Christians make up slightly more than one-third of church members. They are participants. The rest are spectators. Participants choose battles of endurance and persecution. Instead of taking the path of least resistance or bowing to political pressures, they arm themselves with God's Word. They stand on his principles and lay down their lives, reputations, and wealth for Christ. They are ready to turn the world right side up. *Acts 17:6*

God didn't give you the armor listed in Ephesians 6:13–17 so you could sit on the bench and snooze. He wants you to go to war and fight for the cause of Christ and to establish his kingdom on the earth. Are you man enough to step into the spiritual arena? Do you wilt when others mock you and sneer at your faith? Are you ready to pick up the sword of God's Word and fight with that weapon? Are you willing to put your reputation and image aside so you can leave a mark in the sands of time? If you are tired of lukewarm, minor league Christianity and want to enter the majors, the world awaits your influence.

—Tom Sirotnak

YOU DON'T HAVE TO BE A FIST-POUNDING FIREBRAND. BUT TRUST GOD FOR THE BOLDNESS, OPPORTUNITIES, AND WISDOM TO REPRESENT HIS CAUSE WELL WHEREVER HE CALLS YOU.

JEHOSHAPHAT
GODLY GOVERNING

SELECTIONS FROM 2 CHRONICLES 19

There are few bright spots among the kings who littered Israel's landscape between Solomon and the years of captivity. Jehoshaphat, however, is one of them. His high ideals for himself and his officials ring a patriotic cord in all of us who long for godly leadership in government.

Jehoshaphat lived in Jerusalem, and went in and out among the people from Beer-sheba to the hill country of Ephraim, and brought them back to the LORD God of their fathers.

He stationed judges in the land—in all the fortified cities, city by city. Then he said to the judges, "Consider what you are doing, for you do not judge for man, but for the LORD, who is with you in the matter of judgment.

"And now, may the terror of the LORD be on you. Watch what you do, for there is no injustice, nor partiality, nor taking of bribes with the LORD our God."

Of all the factors that led to Jehoshaphat's sound perspectives on government, perhaps the most distinct was his heritage. His desire to continue Asa's noble initiatives makes you think his father had made an effort to do more than just leave behind a good example. You can almost imagine Asa bringing him into the decision rooms, discussing matters of loyalty and leadership on their twilight walks. That's because heritage is a lot more than feats and accomplishments, but time and communication. We owe that to our children.

LOOK AT IT THIS WAY

Our laws and our institutions must necessarily be based upon the teachings of the Redeemer of mankind. It is impossible that it should be otherwise; and in this sense and to this extent, our civilization and our institutions are emphatically Christian.

No purpose of action against religion can be imputed to any legislation, state or national, because this is a religious people. This is historically true. From the discovery of this continent to the present hour, there is a single voice making this affirmation. There is no dissonance in these declarations. There is a universal language pervading them all, having one meaning; they affirm and reaffirm that this is a religious nation. These are not individual sayings, declarations of private persons: they are organic utterances; they speak the voice of the entire people.

The happiness of a people and the good order and preservation of civil government essentially depend upon piety, religion, and morality. Religion, morality, and knowledge are necessary to good government, the preservation of liberty, and the happiness of mankind.

–United States Supreme Court, 1892

NOT MANY OF US WILL HOLD GOVERNMENTAL OFFICE, BUT WE CAN PRAY FOR THOSE WHO DO AND SUPPORT THOSE WHO USE THEIR POSITIONS TO HONOR GOD WITH THEIR ACTIONS AND DECISIONS.

ELISHA
MODELING HIS MENTOR

SELECTIONS FROM 2 KINGS 2

Elisha had felt God's call on his life. But Elijah gave that call a face. Whenever Elisha felt like quitting or telling God he could never live this lonely life of a prophet, he'd see Elijah. He'd see all he ever wanted to be in life. And in the distance he could hear God's call again.

Elijah said to him, "Stay here, please, for the LORD has sent me to the Jordan." But Elisha said, "As the LORD lives, and as your soul lives, I will not leave you." So the two of them went on.

Now 50 men from the sons of the prophets went and stood facing them at a distance from them, while the two of them stood by the Jordan. Then Elijah took his mantle, rolled it up, and struck the waters, and the waters parted to the one side and the other. Then the two of them passed over on dry ground.

When they had crossed over, Elijah said to Elisha, "Ask! What may I do for you before I'm taken from you?" So Elisha said, "Let there be, please, a double portion of your spirit on me."

Basketball teams call him their go-to guy—the one whose track record proves that he can deliver in clutch situations, the one whose attitude and desire raise the whole team's level of performance up a notch. That's what Elijah was for Elisha. He was his spiritual go-to guy. We all need rooted, godly people we can model our lives after, people who can share more over a cup of coffee than we usually get in a whole meal of our own ideas and perceptions. Aren't you just a little bit hungry for that?

LOOK AT IT THIS WAY

Every man should seek to have three individuals in his life.

You need a Paul. That is, you need an older man who is willing to build into your life. You need somebody who's been down the road. Somebody who's willing to share with you not only his strengths, but also his weaknesses.

You also need a Barnabas. That is, you need a soul brother, somebody who loves you, but is not impressed by you. Somebody who is not taken in by your charm and popularity and to whom you can be accountable.

Third, you need a Timothy. You need a younger man into whose life you are building. Paul spoke of the need for somebody who can affirm and encourage you, for somebody who will teach and pray for you, for somebody who will correct and direct you. That's the kind of person young people are looking for.

I can assure you after much experience that you haven't lived as a Christian until you have been mentored. And you haven't known fulfillment until you have been involved in the process of mentoring.

–Howard Hendricks

PRAY ABOUT FINDING A PERSON WHO CAN HOLD YOU ACCOUNTABLE AND OFFER YOU ENCOURAGEMENT, AS WELL AS A PERSON WHO COULD BENEFIT FROM YOUR EXPERIENCE. IT'S A WIN-WIN SITUATION.

ELISHA
SPIRITUAL EYESIGHT

SELECTIONS FROM 2 KINGS 6

A prophet's work was life-threatening. His task of articulating God's dead-steady message across the bow of public sentiment kept him constantly in the line of fire—from foe and countryman alike. But he had a weapon no enemy could calculate: he had spiritual eyesight.

Spend more time in His Word

Now when the man of God's aide rose early in the morning and went out, to his surprise, an army was surrounding the city with horses and chariots. So his servant said to him, "Oh, my lord, what will we do?"

Elisha said, "Don't be afraid, for those who are with us are more than those who are with them."

Then Elisha prayed and said, "O LORD, please open his eyes that he may see." So the LORD opened the young man's eyes and he looked, and to his surprise the mountain was full of horses and chariots of fire surrounding Elisha.

Chances are, you use your spiritual eyesight even more than you realize. Not every spiritual inclination becomes Sunday morning testimony material, but that makes it no less valid. It may just be having someone come to mind. Or reading God's fingerprint into a news event. Your sensibility to the Lord will grow, for sure, as you get closer to him and spend more time in his Word—even more as you practice responding to his voice and expecting his direction. But you're doing it already. In fact, you're working on it right now.

081918

LOOK AT IT THIS WAY

Ancient Israel and the early church both operated on the understanding that their abilities were not all material. They believed that they had at their disposal invisible, immaterial, supernatural forces.

The people of God in Scripture understood that we who do the work of God live in two worlds, the one we can see and the one we cannot. The modern Western church has come to believe itself limited to the same world as the unbeliever. We need the God of glory to open our eyes so that we can see beyond the limitations of our material world.

There is a time to cease rationalizing, to simply bow down before the awesome presence of the eternal God. We must regain piety in the good sense—a humble and wholesome attitude toward sacred things. And we must recover the sacraments—not just the perfunctory observance of them, but we need to learn to pass through them into the court of heaven. They should be windows in the wall of our material world through which we glimpse the glories of the world to come.

–Dan Scott

PART OF THE CHRISTIAN WALK IS LEARNING HOW TO BE QUIET ENOUGH TO LISTEN TO THE SPIRIT'S VOICE. YOU DO IT IN SLOW STEPS, THROUGH PRAYER, BY MAKING MISTAKES, BY LETTING FAITH LEAD THE WAY.

UZZIAH
PULLED DOWN BY PRIDE

SELECTIONS FROM 2 CHRONICLES 26

Success is never enough for some people. Power, privilege—they blind people to their own limits. They render the attainment reflex uncontrollable. That was King Uzziah. He had success—God-given, God-blessed success. But he just couldn't stop himself from wanting more.

When [Uzziah] became strong, his heart grew haughty to his own destruction. He acted unfaithfully against the LORD his God by going into the LORD's sanctuary to burn incense on the incense altar. Azariah the priest, along with 80 valiant priests of the LORD, went in after him. They took their stand against King Uzziah and said, "Uzziah, you have no right to offer incense to the LORD. . . . Get out of the sanctuary! You have acted unfaithfully!". . .

Uzziah, with a censer in his hand to offer incense, was enraged. But when he became enraged with the priests, leprosy broke out on his forehead in the presence of the priests. . . .

King Uzziah was a leper to the day of his death.

Leprosy. The chalky white, emaciated skin. The worn nubs left behind by severed toes and fingers. The horrified, sideways glances from those who were so beneath Uzziah's kingly position. Could there have been a more fitting way to thoroughly pulverize his pride than to be stripped of his appearance, his freedom of movement, his place of honor—even to be too diseased for burial in the royal tombs, being laid to rest instead in a nearby field? Pride can blow a lot of air into our self-concept, but it offers nothing to brace our fall.

LOOK AT IT THIS WAY

Uzziah knew the Scriptures. He knew that God's law strictly forbade anyone to burn incense at that altar but one of the priests. He knew that he was violating the worship of God. But he had become blind. He couldn't even see the old familiar things he had known from childhood.

But that's what arrogance does. You begin to expect certain privileges in your life and feel angry or bitter when they don't fall your way. When you study the surrounding cultures of Uzziah's day, many of the other kings also had the privilege and prerogative of acting as priests. It may be that Uzziah looked around at some of the things his contemporaries were doing and thought, Why can't I be a priest AND a king like these other guys? Are they better than I am? Yet it was a direct violation of God's ways and God's commands. Uzziah knew it, but in his blindness he just couldn't see it anymore.

Uzziah started so well, lived up to so much of his potential, but finished out of the race. Why? Because he got suckered by pride.

—Steve Farrar

BURN AWAY YOUR PRIDE BY CONTINUALLY YIELDING CONTROL OF YOUR THOUGHTS, HABITS, AND ACTIONS TO GOD. NOTHING THAT'S IN YOU WILL EVER DEFEAT IT. THAT WOULD ONLY MAKE YOU PROUDER.

HEZEKIAH
POWERED BY PRAYER

SELECTIONS FROM 2 KINGS 19

Hezekiah knew kings weren't supposed to feel this way. But he was scared. To death. Sennacherib was coming, bringing with him an annihilating promise he had been known to fulfill. Sennacherib! Just the name sounded like a fist in the stomach. Hezekiah's was already in a knot.

[Sennacherib] sent messengers to Hezekiah, saying . . . "Don't let your God in whom you trust deceive you by promising that Jerusalem will not be given into the hand of the king of Assyria. Look, you have heard what the kings of Assyria have done to all the lands, destroying them completely, and will you be delivered? . . .

Hezekiah took the letter from the hand of the messengers and read it. Then he went up to the temple of the LORD and spread it out before the LORD. . . . "O LORD God of Israel . . . hear the words of Sennacherib that he has sent to mock the living God. . . . Save us from his hand, that all the kingdoms of the earth may know that You alone, LORD, are God."

Hezekiah's example offers one of the most descriptive word pictures in the vocabulary of prayer. The Bible says he took the warring king's threatening letter into the temple and "spread it out before the Lord." He knew this was totally out of his control. Perhaps that's why our deepest, most agonizing prayers drive us to a prostrate position. Face down. Arms outstretched. All vulnerabilities exposed. Empty-handed, with all our bright ideas left behind. It's as low as we ever get before God. It's as close as we ever get to his heart.

LOOK AT IT THIS WAY

Because of a very dense fog, the captain had remained on the bridge continuously for twenty-four hours when George Mueller came to him and said, "Sir, I have come to tell you that I must be in Quebec on Saturday afternoon." When he was informed that it was impossible, he replied, "Very well, if the ship cannot take me, God will find some other way. Let us go down to the chart room and pray."

" 'Mr. Mueller,' I said, 'do you not know how dense the fog is?' "

" 'No,' he replied, 'my eye is not on the density of the fog, but on the living God who controls every circumstance of my life.' He knelt down and prayed a simple prayer. I looked at him, and he said, 'Get up and open the door and you will find that the fog is gone.' "

"I got up, and indeed the fog was gone. George Mueller was in Quebec Saturday afternoon for his engagement. I learned from that man that if you know God and if you know his will for your life, and circumstances seem impossible, pray believing that God will—and he will!"

—Norman Harrison

WHEN'S THE LAST TIME YOU CRIED OUT TO GOD—WHEN YOU SPREAD EVERYTHING OUT BEFORE HIM AND TOTALLY SUBMITTED TO HIS WILL? THERE'S REST AND RELEASE WAITING DOWN THERE ON THE CARPET.

JOSIAH
RENEWING THE COVENANT

SELECTIONS FROM 2 CHRONICLES 34

It had been years since Israelite families had celebrated their prescribed feasts or united in worship to something besides a carved rock or a piece of wood. God's distinguishing marks were all but gone from his people—till one king found a light in the dark ages.

When they brought out the money that had been deposited in the LORD's temple, Hilkiah the priest found the book of the law of the LORD written by the hand of Moses. . . . Shaphan took the book to the king . . . and Shaphan read it to the king.

When the king heard the words of the law, he tore his clothes. . . . So the king sent messengers, and gathered all the elders of Judah and Jerusalem. Then the king went up to the LORD's temple. . . . Next the king stood at his post and made a covenant in the LORD's presence to follow the LORD and to keep His commandments, His decrees, and His statutes with all his heart and with all his soul in order to carry out the words of the covenant written in this book.

Some historians cast a skeptical eye on this event in Israel's history. They propose that Josiah was coerced by the priests to go along with this scheme of "finding" (wink, wink) a divinely written scroll, thus throwing the weight of God behind their programs of reinvigorating national morality. There will always be those who cast doubt on the Bible, who roll their eyes at God's people and explain away his work. You're not likely to convince them by argument. But if they'll only believe what they see, let them see a faithful follower in you.

LOOK AT IT THIS WAY

If you want to begin praying for revival in the nation, start by seeking revival in your own heart, and let revival begin in you. Our only hope for a future in our nation is for revival to sweep our churches and spiritual awakening to touch the land. If our nation is to return to the Lord and fear him once again, God's people must begin the repentance.

We must meet God's requirements. We must deal ruthlessly with our stubborn pride, and humble ourselves before the Lord. Then we must pray and seek his face. Prayer is a relationship with a person. Prayer is entering into the throne room of the universe to stand before the Lord God Almighty. When God's people take prayer seriously and enter the presence of Holy God, they will recognize their sin, and fall with broken and contrite hearts before his majesty.

When we come to understand the nature of our sin, and when we have a broken heart about it, we will be ready to repent and return to the Lord. God stands ready to grant and enable our repentance, if we will just respond to his invitation.

—Henry Blackaby

RIGHT NOW MIGHT BE A GOOD TIME IN LIFE FOR YOU TO STOP AND THINK—TO SEE HOW CLOSE YOU'RE WALKING TO THE TRUTHS YOU PROFESS. RENEW YOUR PRIORITIES IN LIGHT OF GOD'S WORD.

EZRA

LOVE FOR GOD'S WORD

SELECTIONS FROM EZRA 7

With a Bible in every room, we have no way of understanding how precious that scroll was to Ezra. We probably don't even have a way to feel the full weight of those precious words in the same way he did. When he read them, everyone knew he was doing what he loved.

On the first day of the first month, he began the journey from Babylon, and on the first day of the fifth month he arrived in Jerusalem, because his God's gracious hand was on him. For Ezra had determined in his heart to study the law of the LORD, to obey it, and to teach its statutes and ordinances to Israel. . . .

When the seventh month came, the Israelites were in their towns, and all the people gathered together as one at the square in front of the Water Gate. They asked Ezra the scribe to bring the book of the law of Moses that the LORD had commanded Israel. . . . He read out of it from daybreak until noon before the men, the women, and those who could understand.

Have you ever heard people tell how—from fatigue, sleeplessness, or some other disorientation—they were driving their car, arrived at their destination, and suddenly realized that they had no recollection of the trip? Is that the way Bible reading has become for you? You sit down, you start off a chapter, then you look up five minutes later with no idea what you've just read? Try Ezra's way, then. Try reading the Bible aloud next time, adding your ears as a member of the audience, and see if you don't enjoy the ride a lot more.

LOOK AT IT THIS WAY

Living among the Chaldeans, who were famous for the study of literature and astronomy, perhaps made it difficult for Ezra to prefer to study the law of the Lord. But he sought the law of the Lord; he made it his business to search the Scriptures and to inquire into the knowledge of God. He knew that he could find the knowledge and the will of God in the Scriptures, but he also knew that he would not find it without seeking for it. So he prepared his heart to do it; he took pains in his studies; and he became a ready scribe.

After being instrumental in reviving the knowledge of God among the captive Jews in Babylon, Ezra went to Jerusalem to teach Israel. He offered "to teach in Israel the statutes and judgments" of God's law, for he was willing to share what he had learned for the good of others. You will observe, however, that he first learned and then he taught; he first practiced the commandments himself and then directed others in the practice of them. His example confirmed his doctrine.

—Matthew Henry

LOVE FOR GOD'S WORD IS ONLY FOUND IN HIS WORD— AS YOU READ IT AND STUDY IT WITH MORE FAITHFULNESS THAN ANY OTHER BOOK OR ATTRACTION. MARK IT DOWN. AND DO IT EVERY DAY.

NEHEMIAH
UNPOLLUTED BY POWER

SELECTIONS FROM NEHEMIAH 5

Nehemiah was in charge, which meant that all the privileges of power were his to enjoy. But he had learned a concept Jesus would later put into words: "Whoever wants to be first among you must be a slave to all" (Mark 10:44). Nehemiah would join him in putting it into practice.

From the day that King Artaxerxes appointed me to be their governor in the land of Judah, from the twentieth year until his thirty-second year—12 years—neither I nor my associates ever ate from the food allotted to the governor. The former governors, my predecessors, had heavily burdened the people, taking food and wine from them, as well as a pound of silver. Their subordinates also oppressed the people.

But I didn't do this, because of the fear of God. Instead, I devoted myself to the work on the wall. All my subordinates were gathered there for the work. We didn't buy any property. . . . Remember me favorably, my God, for all that I have done for the people.

Write it down. This is just God's way. Those who are seeking his will for their lives—and who find it in noticeable positions of prominence—are those he's been able to trust with the ordinary and obscure. The principle that Christ taught in the parable of the talents will always hold true. "You were faithful over a few things; I will put you in charge of many things" (Matthew 25:21). If we'll concentrate on doing well what is right in front of us, God will open the door to fulfillment when we're ready for it.

LOOK AT IT THIS WAY

Nehemiah was motivated by three factors as he carried out his work as governor. He feared God, he was sensitive to people's needs, and he desired God's special blessing in his life. If we approach advancement and promotion with these same basic motivations, we, too, will have the key to maintaining our spiritual and psychological equilibrium.

Today, we need more godly fear. We should stand in awe of who God is and what he's done for us—and that eventually we will have to give an account to him for how we have lived our lives on earth.

If we are sensitive to others, we'll not take advantage of them. We'll never use our positions of power to exploit them. Rather, we'll use these opportunities to help people—to make their lives more comfortable and to create better living and working conditions. Our goal will be like that of Christ—to become a greater servant as our position of authority and power increases. When we are motivated by this kind of thinking, we'll be able to handle almost any promotion without succumbing to Satan's tactics.

—Gene Getz

EVEN THE SEDUCTION OF POWER CAN'T FOOL YOU WHEN YOUR HEART IS FIXED ON PLEASING THE LORD. BE A PERSON WHO'S NOT AS WORRIED ABOUT WHAT YOU DESERVE AS WHO YOU SERVE.

MORDECAI
ADVOCATE FOR THE OPPRESSED

SELECTIONS FROM ESTHER 3 & 4

If you want to find Mordecai in the story of Esther, look for him out in the street—with one ear on his people's concerns and the other on the rumors streaming from the palace—rumors of a plot to destroy them. With Mordecai, the Jewish people had a fighting chance.

Haman informed King Xerxes, "There is one ethnic group, scattered throughout the peoples in every province of your kingdom, yet living in isolation. Their laws are different from everyone else's, so they defy the king's laws. It's not in the king's best interest to guarantee their security. If the king approves, let an order be drawn up authorizing their destruction. That being done, I will weigh out 375 tons of silver in the hands of the accountants to be deposited in the royal treasury."...

When Mordecai learned all that had occurred, he tore his clothes, put on sackcloth and ashes, went into the middle of the city, and cried aloud bitterly.

Isaiah 58 is one of the Bible's most probing examinations of the believer's heart. Speaking God's words, the prophet takes on the proud proponents of religious observance—those who are sure that God couldn't be more pleased with their rituals and righteousness. Isaiah reveals that going without food means little while the oppressed go hungry, that wearing sackcloth only makes you itchy if the naked remain unclothed. God's heart is for the helpless, and his people don't really know him if they aren't actively helping them.

LOOK AT IT THIS WAY

Eventually every nation in every age must be judged by this test: How did it treat people? The great dramatic moments of history have left us with monuments and memories of compassion, love, and unselfishness which punctuate the all-too-pervasive malevolence that dominates so much of human interaction. That there is any respite from evil is due to some courageous people who, on the basis of personal philosophies, have led campaigns against the ill-treatment and misuse of individuals. Each era faces its own unique blend of problems. Our own time is no exception. Those who regard individuals as expendable raw material—to be molded, exploited, and then discarded—do battle on many fronts with those who see each person as unique and special, worthwhile, and irreplaceable.

There are choices to be made in every age. And who we are depends on the choices we make. What will our choices be? What boundaries will we uphold to make it possible for people to say with certainty that moral atrocities are evil? Which side will we be on?

—Francis Schaeffer

YOU CAN'T CHAMPION EVERY CAUSE, BUT YOU CAN VISIT A NURSING HOME. YOU CAN WRITE A LETTER. YOU CAN SKIP A MEAL AND FEED A BEGGAR. DON'T WAIT FOR ANOTHER GUILT TRIP. GO AHEAD AND CATCH THIS ONE.

HAMAN
PRISONER TO PREJUDICE

SELECTIONS FROM ESTHER 3 & 5

Haman didn't just say the word Jew. He spit it. It came out with a venom his heart couldn't contain. They were pests. They were appalling. They were in his way. And he was going to rid his land of them if it was the last thing he did. Poor Haman— he had to leave his plans hanging.

When Haman saw that Mordecai was not bowing down or paying him homage, he was filled with rage. Haman hated to punish just Mordecai by himself. Having learned of Mordecai's ethnic identity, Haman set out to destroy all the Jewish people—Mordecai's people—throughout all of Xerxes's kingdom. . . .

Haman got himself under control and went home. He sent for his friends and Zeresh, his wife, to join him. . . . He told them all about how the king had promoted him in rank and given him a high position over the other officials and the royal staff. . . . "Still, none of this satisfies me since I see Mordecai the Jew sitting at the King's Gate all the time."

Do you know the rest of this story? The gallows that Haman had built for Mordecai would feel the weight of his own hate instead. But isn't that always the way with prejudice? Those who possess its poison inside are the ones who really suffer. It breaks down their relationships, distorts their perspectives, and stands like a stiff-arm between them and God. And in trying to justify their principles of prejudice, they come off looking as foolish as Haman did, falling all over himself on his way to a fool's grave.

LOOK AT IT THIS WAY

The first thing that happens after we have realized our election to God in Christ Jesus is the destruction of our prejudices, parochial notions, and patriotisms; we are turned into servants of God's own purpose.

Our Lord never nurses our prejudices. He mortifies them, runs clean athwart them. We imagine that God has a special interest in our particular prejudices; we are quite sure that God will never deal with us as he has to deal with other people. But instead of God being on the side of our prejudices, he is deliberately wiping them out. It is part of our moral education to have our prejudices run straight across by his providence. God pays no respect to anything we bring to him. There is only one thing God wants of us, and that is our unconditional surrender.

When once we realize that through the salvation of Jesus Christ we are made perfectly fit for God, we shall understand why Jesus Christ is so ruthless in his demands. He demands absolute rectitude from his servants, because he has put into them the very nature of God.

—Oswald Chambers

EVEN IN ITS SMALL, ACCEPTABLE FORMS IN SOCIETY, PREJUDICE LEAVES BITES THAT CAN STING FOR A LONG TIME. SO ASK YOURSELF THIS HARD QUESTION: "IS THERE PREJUDICE INSIDE ME?" NOW ASK ANOTHER ONE: "WHY?"

JOB
FAITH THAT LASTS

SELECTIONS FROM JOB 16 & 19

Job's patience is legendary. Even those who give little thought to the things of God know a little of his story. But those who know better can hang around long enough to see more than the patience of Job. They'll see that perseverance is pointless unless your hope has a Name.

"God has delivered me to unjust men; He has thrown me into the hands of wicked men. I was at ease, but He shattered me; He seized me by the scruff of the neck and smashed me to pieces. He set me up to use as His own target. . . .

"My face has grown red with weeping; death's dark shadow covers my eyelids, although I have not resorted to violence, and my prayer has been pure. . . .

"But I know that my Redeemer lives, and that finally He will stand on the dust, and after my skin has been stripped off in this way, yet in my flesh I will see God, whom I will see for myself. Yes, my own eyes will see, and not a stranger."

When you're going through a difficult time, it's nice to have friends. Unless, of course, your friends are like Job's. But even with all their pious ramblings, who knows how much harder it would have been on Job if he'd had to endure his trial alone? At least they were there. His other friends didn't even show. Sometimes we may stop short of reaching out to someone who's hurting, not sure what to say or how to show our concern. But almost always, it's not our words but just our presence that does the caring.

LOOK AT IT THIS WAY

Thou hast enlarged me when I was in distress"
(Psalm 4:1, KJV). The more one thinks of these words,
the more they reveal their wonderful meaning. Darby
renders it, "In pressure, Thou hast enlarged me," and
Kay, "In straits Thou madest wide room for me."
Whatever the pressure be, in that pressure—think of
it—enlargement; the very opposite of what the word
"pressure" suggests. And room, plenty of room, in a
strait place.

We may sometimes feel distressed: here then is a
word of pure hope and consolation. Largeness, like
the largeness of the sea, is his gift to us. We shall not
be flattened in spirit by pressure, but enlarged. In the
narrow ways of pain or of temptation, he will make
wide room for us. In Job's deepest despondency, he
wished to be as he was when "the intimacy of God
was over [his] tent" (Job 29:4, KJV), and he did not
know that, even then, he was very near to a more
wonderful intimacy than had ever been his before. Is
it not joyful to think that it may be so with us? Today,
even today, we may be on the verge of—what?

—Amy Carmichael

THERE ARE TIMES WHEN, EVEN WITH ALL THE BIBLE WORDS IN THE WORLD, THERE'S NO ANSWER FOR WHAT YOU'RE FACING . . . EXCEPT ONE: JESUS. CLING TO HIM. HE'S THE ONLY HOPE YOU'VE GOT.

ISAIAH
FEARING GOD

SELECTIONS FROM ISAIAH 6

You've heard this passage preached time and time again. But no matter how many approaches you take, one thing is unmistakable: Isaiah saw something awesome. "Awesome" is not your kind of word? Then how about numbing, staggering, breathtaking. Feel it all over again.

In the year that King Uzziah died, I saw the Lord seated on a high and lofty throne, and His robe filled the temple. Seraphim were standing above Him; each one had six wings: with two he covered his face, with two he covered his feet, and with two he flew. And one called to another: "Holy, holy, holy is the LORD of Hosts; His glory fills the whole earth." The foundations of the doorways shook at the sound of their voices, and the temple was filled with smoke.

Then I said: "Woe is me, for I am ruined because I am a man of unclean lips and live among a people of unclean lips, and because my eyes have seen the King, the LORD of Hosts."

Uzziah had been king for what seemed like forever, longer than any other person in Jewish history. He was certainly the only king Isaiah had ever known. And his death—no matter how expected at such an advanced age—had to rattle a deep chord of disbelief. Uzziah, dead! It seemed impossible. This had to be Isaiah's mood the day God shuddered him to his socks with the painful brilliance of his presence. When everything stable had suddenly been shaken, God gave Isaiah a glimpse of the unshakable. And Isaiah never forgot it.

LOOK AT IT THIS WAY

In olden days, men of faith were said to "walk in the fear of God." However intimate their communion with God, however bold their prayers, at the base of their religious life was the conception of God as awesome and dreadful. The idea of God transcendent runs through the whole Bible and gives color and tone to the character of the saints.

Whenever God appeared to men in Bible times, the results were the same—an overwhelming sense of terror and dismay, a wrenching sensation of sinfulness and guilt. When God spoke, Abram stretched himself upon the ground to listen. When Moses saw the Lord in the burning bush, he hid his face in fear to look upon God. Isaiah's vision of God wrung from him the cry, "Woe is me!" and the confession, "I am undone; because I am a man of unclean lips."

These experiences show that a vision of the divine transcendence soon ends all controversy between the man and his God. The fight goes out of the man and he is ready with the conquered Saul to ask meekly, "Lord, what wilt thou have me to do?"

—A. W. Tozer

SOMETIME SOON, GO TO YOUR FAVORITE, QUIETEST, HOLIEST PLACE. AND SPEND ENOUGH TIME THERE TILL YOU FEEL GOD'S PRESENCE OVER YOU, AROUND YOU, BEHIND YOU. HE'S AWESOME, ISN'T HE?

JEREMIAH
OBEDIENCE TO HIS CALLING

SELECTIONS FROM JEREMIAH 20

There were days when Jeremiah would have given anything to be someone else, because this call was costing him everything. His friends. His reputation. Perhaps even his life, if some people had their way. But the fire he feared most was the one that burned inside of him.

"I am a laughingstock all the time; everyone ridicules me. For whenever I speak, I cry out. I proclaim, "Violence and devastation!" For the word of the Lord has become for me constant humiliation and derision.

"If I say, 'I will not mention Him, nor speak any longer in His name,' His message becomes a fire burning in my heart, shut up in my bones. I become tired of holding it in, and I cannot prevail.

"For I have heard the gossip of the multitudes, 'Terror is all around! Report him; let's report him!' Everyone I trusted watches for my fall. . . . But the Lord is with me like a violent warrior . . . for to You I have disclosed my case."

Jeremiah's main beef was with the religious and political establishment of his day, the priests and rulers who shouldered the responsibility for serving God's people and inspiring them to holiness. In their grasp for power—and the grip of their own sin—they had lost the credibility and discernment to lead as God desired. "They dress the wound of my people as though it were not serious," Jeremiah would say. And still today, when immorality and pride masquerades as authority, the wounds go untreated. Sin escalates. Pain perseveres.

LOOK AT IT THIS WAY

We do all as unto the Lord and not unto other people. We live with our Lord in view. We look always to the "author and finisher of our faith" (Hebrews 12:1–2, NKJV). When our focus is on people and whether they follow us, respond favorably to us, affirm us, or recognize us with gifts and praise, we are courting pain and disappointment. Our peace in ministry comes from a strong and clear relationship with God. He gives the affirmation; he provides his love—and this is enough!

God's wonderful provision for life at God's best is a life lived in, controlled by, and responsive to the Holy Spirit's presence and power. What we cannot do, he can and will do. No one can make me angry when the Holy Spirit is controlling me. Nothing can disturb the peace of God in me when he is in control of me.

Deliberately cultivating the life of the Son of God in me is crucial to peace and contentment in my life and ministry. When my life is lived with his peace, then I can lead others to experience his peace as well.

—Henry Blackaby

EXPECT SOME MAJOR-LEAGUE CHALLENGES TO THE CALLING GOD HAS PLACED ON YOUR LIFE. AND WHEN YOU FEEL LIKE QUITTING, TAKE IT AS A WARNING THAT YOU'RE TRYING TO DO TOO MUCH BY YOURSELF.

SHADRACH, MESHACH & ABEDNEGO

NO COMPROMISE

SELECTIONS FROM DANIEL 3

Imagine being in a sold-out stadium with thousands of ravenous hometown fans, and you're one of the few who are wearing the opponent's colors. That was the situation for these three Hebrew boys. But nothing was going to keep them from standing up for their side.

> "You, the king, have issued a decree that everyone who hears the sound of the horn, flute, zither, lyre, harp, drum, and every kind of music must fall down and worship the gold statue. . . . These men have ignored you, the king; they do not serve your gods or worship the gold statue you have set up."
>
> Then Nebuchadnezzar in a furious rage gave orders to bring in Shadrach, Meshach, and Abednego. . . . "Nebuchadnezzar . . . if the God we serve exists, then He can rescue us from the furnace of blazing fire, and He can rescue us from the power of you the king. But even if He does not rescue us, we want you, the king, to know that we will not serve your gods or worship the gold statue you set up."

These three were part of a select group of young Hebrew boys who were deported from their homeland and conscripted as leadership trainees in the courts of Babylon. It was a practice that stripped Israel of her brightest and best, but it couldn't strip away the heritage of those who had been raised to worship the one true God. Our children face a world with ample opportunities for compromise. But by building a base of truth and Christian character beneath them, we can strengthen their inclination for sound, moral choices.

LOOK AT IT THIS WAY

A somewhat common practice in the business world is to consider people who take a stand for issues of conscience as suspect, as threatening, or even perhaps as losers who should be passed over by others who are more willing to play the game. I truly believe that taking a stand for issues of character, honesty, and fair practice will, in the long run, cause one to prosper in all the right ways. However, if one is going to be a man or woman of integrity, one needs to realize that it may, in the short run, be very costly.

I know people who have gone through difficult situations and are bitter at God for not rescuing them from their own fiery furnaces. They feel as though the Lord abandoned them. They feel justified in their moral lapses because God didn't come through for them as they thought he should. These three young friends of Daniel's were committed to do what was right without respect to the outcome—whether it benefited them or cost them everything. They so greatly valued their integrity, they were willing to pay the ultimate price to stand for what was right.

—Jim Henry

THE PRESSURE TO CONFORM IS A CONDITION YOU NEVER OUTGROW. BUT WITH PRACTICE, YOU CAN BUILD ENOUGH BIBLICAL BOUNDARIES AROUND YOURSELF TO STAND UP TO THE MOST COMPROMISING SITUATIONS.

DANIEL
FAITHFULNESS WITHOUT REWARD

SELECTIONS FROM DANIEL 5

Think fast, Belshazzar! Put yourself in Daniel's shoes. If you were the wise man, bearing critical information of interest to the crown, what would you want in return? Riches? Yes, and recognition. Maybe a new title for your business card. Daniel says no? What is it this guy wants?

King Belshazzar held a great feast for 1,000 of his nobles. . . . At that moment the fingers of a man's hand appeared and began writing on the plaster of the king's palace wall next to the lampstand.

Daniel was brought before the king. . . . "I have heard about you that you can give interpretations and solve problems. Therefore, if you can read this inscription and give me its interpretation, you will be clothed in purple, have a gold chain around your neck, and have the third highest position in the kingdom." Then Daniel answered the king, "You may keep your gifts, and give your rewards to someone else; however, I will read the inscription for the king and make the interpretation known to him."

Daniel had been in this spot before, as a junior member of Nebuchadnezzar's mystical advisory board. When the king had ordered an axe to every one of their necks for failing to interpret his dream, Daniel was the only one with a true God to consult and the only one brave enough to give the king a less-than-pleasant report. Spiritual growth builds on spiritual experience. And like Daniel, our confidence in following the Lord's nudgings will grow as we get used to the sound of his voice.

LOOK AT IT THIS WAY

Faithfulness is consecration in overalls. It is the steady acceptance and performance of the common duty and the immediate task without any reference to personal preferences—because it is there to be done and so is a manifestation of the will of God.

Faithfulness means continuing quietly with the job we have been given, in the situation where we have been placed, not yielding to the restless desire for change. It means tending the lamp quietly for God without wondering how much longer it has got to go on. Steady, unsensational driving, taking good care of the car. It means keeping everything in your charge in good order for love's sake, rubbing up the silver, polishing the glass even though you know the Master will not be looking round the pantry next weekend.

If your life is really part of the apparatus of the Spirit, that is the sort of life it must be. You have got to be the sort of cat who can be left alone with the canary: the sort of dog who follows, hungry and thirsty but tail up, to the very end of the day.

—Evelyn Underhill

WOULD YOU WORK HARDER FOR MORE PAY? MORE RESPONSIBILITY? A COMPANY CAR? IF PERKS DON'T TURN YOUR HEAD, THEN YOU CAN BE PRETTY SURE THAT YOU'RE WORKING FOR ALL THE RIGHT REASONS.

JONAH
RUNNING FROM GOD

SELECTIONS FROM JONAH 1

Street preaching has never been an easy job, and anyone who is called to it must come equipped with a thick-skinned hide for unholy accusations and feet that are able to stand toe-to-toe with the nastiest dissenters. But when Jonah got the call, his feet just weren't in it.

The word of the LORD came to Jonah son of Amittai: "Get up! Go to the great city of Nineveh and preach against it, because their wickedness has come up before Me." However, Jonah got up to flee to Tarshish away from the LORD's presence. He went down to Joppa and found a ship going to Tarshish. . . .

Then the LORD hurled a violent wind onto the sea, and such a violent storm came up on the sea that the ship threatened to break apart. . . . They said to him, "What should we do to you to calm this sea that's against us?". . . He answered them, "Pick me up and throw me into the sea so that it may quiet down for you, for I know I'm to blame for this violent storm that's against you."

Jonah ran into some stiff head winds during his flight from God's orders. That's because God's mercy and love don't always dress in their nicest clothes. Sometimes God loves us as he did Jonah—with hardship. He knows that his plans hold our only hope for joy and fulfillment. He further knows that when our own plans dwindle into disarray, we will turn to him with a passion we might never have known had it not been for his love showing up in a less than a favorable light—and making everything make sense again.

LOOK AT IT THIS WAY

After you give yourself to the Lord, he begins to break what is offered to him. Everything seems to go wrong, and you protest and find fault with the ways of God. But to stay there is to be no more than just a broken vessel—no good for the world, because you have gone too far for the world to use you, and no good for God either, because you have not gone far enough for him to use you. You are out of gear with the world, and you have a controversy with God. This is the tragedy of many a Christian.

My giving of myself to the Lord must be an initial fundamental act. Then, day by day, I must go on giving to him, not finding fault with his use of me, but accepting with praise even what the flesh finds hard.

I am the Lord's, and now I no longer reckon myself to be my own, but acknowledge in everything His ownership and authority. That is the attitude God delights in, and to maintain it is true consecration. May we always be possessed by the consciousness that we are not our own.

—Watchman Nee

HABAKKUK

TRUSTING GOD ANYWAY

SELECTIONS FROM HABAKKUK 1 & 3

Judah was enjoying the glorious fruit of Josiah's social reforms. Meanwhile, Assyria—once the scourge of the Middle East—was only a shadow of its former self. But now, muddying the carpet of peace and promise, were the barbarous Babylonians. "How long, O Lord?"

"How long, LORD, must I call for help and You not listen, or cry out to You about violence and You not save? Why do You force me to look at injustice? Why do You tolerate wrongdoing? Oppression and violence are right in front of me. Strife is ongoing, and conflict escalates. . . . I trembled where I stood. Now I must quietly wait for the day of distress to come against the people invading us.

"Though the fig tree does not bud and there is no yield on the vines, though the olive crop fails and the fields produce no food, though there are no sheep in the pen and no cattle in the stalls, yet I will exult in the LORD; I will rejoice in the God of my salvation!"

Your boss may think you're a nut for believing in God. Trust God anyway. Your spouse may think you carry your faith a little too far. Trust God anyway. Your family may think you're cushioning yourself and your children from the real world. Trust God anyway. Your health may be failing. Trust God anyway. Your stress may be unbearable. Trust God anyway. Your career track may seem like it's on a slow train to nowhere. Trust God anyway. To make it in this Christian life, there's only one way. And it's to trust God. Anyway.

LOOK AT IT THIS WAY

Habakkuk 2:4 describes the person who can survive such testing times. "See, he is puffed up; his desires are not upright—but the righteous will live by his faith." The person in the right relation to God and to his fellows will live by simply being faithful. That is, people will live by faithfully doing every day what in faith they were accustomed to doing. The formula for survival in hard times is faithful humility—standing under the load, as the New Testament puts it. That is why the righteous outlive the tyrants.

The Book of Habakkuk represents the kind of faith that became the norm for Judaism and later for Christianity. Israel no longer had the means to try to shape their own destiny. Under the empires, they were the passive recipients of whatever good or evil the powerful chose to give them. But in faith they could believe that God, through those whom he allowed to rule, would provide what was necessary for his people to serve God. Believing and waiting became essential elements in their way of life. It should still be so.

—from the *Holman Bible Handbook*

MAKE UP YOUR MIND THAT NOTHING WILL EVER MAKE YOU DOUBT THE REALITY OF GOD, THE HOPE OF HIS ETERNAL KINGDOM, AND THE PROMISE THAT HE IS WORKING ALL THINGS FOR YOUR GOOD.

ZACHARIAH
QUESTIONING GOD

SELECTIONS FROM LUKE 1

Zachariah was an old man. His idea of excitement was watching an auburn sunset bathe the Judean hillsides in fiery light or swapping stories with his friends around the temple. Won't he be dumbfounded to find out—at his age—that he's going to be a first-time daddy?

There was a priest of Abijah's division named Zachariah. . . . He was chosen by lot, according to the custom of the priesthood, to enter the sanctuary of the Lord and burn incense. . . . An angel of the Lord appeared to him. . . . "Do not be afraid, Zachariah, because your prayer has been heard. Your wife Elizabeth will bear you a son, and you will name him John.". . .

"How can I know this?" Zachariah asked the angel. "For I am an old man, and my wife is well along in years." The angel answered him . . . "You will become silent and unable to speak until the day these things take place, because you did not believe my words, which will be fulfilled in their proper time."

Your prayer has been heard, Zachariah. *Prayer? What prayer?* Oh, he had prayed himself blue in the face back when Elizabeth was of childbearing age. For forty years or more he had prayed. But after a while, you just resign yourself to the facts. Wonder how long God had been saving that prayer—like a letter folded up in his breast pocket, waiting for just the right time to answer it? If he'd answered it any sooner, no one would have paid attention. *So Elizabeth is expecting? Well, it's about time.* But this way, it was about God.

LOOK AT IT THIS WAY

Doubt is not the opposite of faith but an element of faith. I have faith that there is an all-loving God in spite of the fact that I have no sure way of knowing that there is.

In short, we look at the world and conclude from what we find that, all evidence to the contrary notwithstanding, we will, like Pascal, place our wager on God. Our faith is that wager.

We can take great heart from Paul's words to the Corinthians that although now we see only through a glass darkly, there will come a day when we will see face to face and understand even as we are fully understood. It is the nature of faith to look beyond itself—and beyond the doubts that must always exist in tension with it, if it is a living faith—to a time on the far side of time when the holy dream is at last revealed to be reality, and all that we take now for reality glimmers like a dream. In the meanwhile, faith is the way we have of seeing while we have only the dark glass to see through.

—Frederick Buechner

WHEN GOD'S WORD ASKS YOU TO BELIEVE SOMETHING THAT'S SIMPLY BEYOND BELIEF, THEN YOU GET TO DECIDE: WILL YOU TRUST YOUR FIVE SENSES OR HAVE SENSE ENOUGH JUST TO BELIEVE HIM?

JOSEPH
STAYING IN GOD'S WILL

SELECTIONS FROM MATTHEW 1

He knew that he hadn't—he hoped and prayed that she hadn't—this just couldn't be happening. Still, Mary had never been known to lie to him before. What's a nice guy like Joseph doing in a mess like this? To help us see the miracles that occur inside the walls of God's will.

The birth of Jesus Christ came about this way: After His mother Mary had been engaged to Joseph, it was discovered before they came together that she was pregnant by means of the Holy Spirit. So Joseph, her husband, being a righteous man, and not wanting to disgrace her publicly, decided to divorce her secretly.

But after he had considered these things, an angel of the Lord —suddenly appeared to him in a dream, saying, "Joseph, son of David, don't be afraid to take Mary as your wife, because what has been conceived in her is by the Holy Spirit. She will give birth to a son, and you are to name Him Jesus, because He will save His people from their sins."

Does God ever speak to you in dreams? The Bible certainly bears out the practice. Joseph did, Jacob did, Nebuchadnezzar, and others. Job's friend, Elihu, said: "God does speak in one way, then in another, but a person may not notice it. In a dream, a vision of the night, when a deep sleep falls upon people amid slumber on their bed" (Job 33:14–15). Certainly dreams are often born from the day's events or from pizza eaten too late at night. But stay open to God's communicating through your dreams. It's been done before.

LOOK AT IT THIS WAY

Many of us want God to speak to us and give us an assignment. However, we are not interested in making any major adjustments in our lives. Biblically, that is impossible. Every time God spoke to people in Scripture about something He wanted to do through them, major adjustments were necessary. They had to adjust their lives to God. Once the adjustments were made, God accomplished his purposes through those he called.

Adjustments may be required in one or more of the following areas: in your circumstances (like job, home, finances), your relationships (family, friends, business associates), your thinking (prejudices, methods, your potential), your commitments (to family, church, job, plans, tradition), your actions (how you pray, give, serve), your beliefs (about God, his purposes, his ways, your relationship to him). The list could go on an on. To go from your ways, thoughts, and purposes to God's will always requires a major adjustment. Once you have made the necessary adjustments, you can follow God in obedience.

–Henry Blackaby

GOD'S WORK IS BIGGER THAN ANY ONE PERSON, YET IT IS PERFORMED THROUGH A GOD-GUIDED NETWORK OF INDIVIDUALS WHO ARE WILLING TO SWIM THE CURRENTS OF HIS WILL. ARE YOU?

SIMEON
NEVER STOP WAITING

SELECTIONS FROM LUKE 2

Most of us would have given up on God years before. But you get the feeling that Simeon never lost hope in God's promise. If he was to see the Messiah in his lifetime, then God was just going to have to extend his lifetime. And Simeon would be there waiting.

There was a man in Jerusalem whose name was Simeon. This man was righteous and devout, looking forward to Israel's consolation, and the Holy Spirit was upon him. It had been revealed to him by the Holy Spirit that he would not see death before he saw the Lord's Messiah. . . .

When the parents brought in the child Jesus to perform for Him what was customary under the law, Simeon took Him up in his arms, praised God, and said: "Now, Master, You can dismiss Your slave in peace, according to Your word. For my eyes have seen Your salvation, which You have prepared in the presence of all peoples— a light for revelation to the Gentiles and glory to Your people Israel."

Waiting requires trust. To stand on a rainy sidewalk waiting for your wife to pick you up after work is to trust that she'll be there as soon as she can. To wait for the start of football season is to trust that, come September, your favorite team will be teeing it up. For Simeon, waiting didn't mean he knew exactly what he was waiting for. There were no three-simple-steps for spotting the Messiah. His motivation for waiting was based on one thing alone. He trusted God. And that made it worth the wait.

LOOK AT IT THIS WAY

The Lord graciously laid me aside once in my life for a number of months and put me, spiritually, into utter darkness. It was almost as though he had forsaken me, almost as though nothing was going on and I had really come to the end of everything. And then by degrees, he brought things back again.

We cannot face the thought that God will keep us aside for so long a time; we cannot bear to wait. And of course, I cannot tell you how long he will take. It will seem as though nothing is happening; as though everything you valued is slipping from your grasp. There confronts you a blank wall with no door in it. Seemingly, everyone is being blessed and used, while you yourself have been passed by and are losing out.

Lie quiet. All is in darkness, but it is only for a night. It must indeed be a full night, but that is all. Afterwards, you will find that everything is given back to you in glorious resurrection; and nothing can measure the difference between what was before and what now is!

—Watchman Nee

WAITING DOESN'T COME WITH INSTRUCTIONS, SHORTCUTS, AND HIGH ADVENTURE. BUT WHAT IT LACKS IN FUN, IT MAKES UP FOR IN FULFILLMENT. GOD'S BLESSINGS COME TO THOSE WHO WAIT IN FAITH.

JOHN THE BAPTIST
THE SUPPORTING ROLE

SELECTIONS FROM JOHN 1

Less under-
standing
philosophers
might look
at the story of
John the Baptist
and say life
was cruel to
him, that he
was forced to
cross a fatal
line in history
that short-
circuited his
effectiveness
and ruined his
search for per-
sonal meaning
and purpose.
What do they
know?

This is John's testimony when the Jews from Jerusalem sent priests and Levites to ask him, "Who are you?" He confessed and did not deny, declaring, "I am not the Messiah. . . . I am a 'voice of one crying out in the wilderness: Make straight the way of the Lord'—just as Isaiah the prophet said. . . .

"I baptize with water," John answered them. "But among you stands Someone you don't know. He is the One coming after me, whose sandal strap I'm not worthy to untie.". . .

The next day John saw Jesus coming toward him and said, "Here is the Lamb of God, who takes away the sin of the world! This is the One I told you about."

Let's look at this a different way. We're used to hearing the sermon about not seeking the spotlight. So even when we're tempted to want a taste of the glory, we're usually smart enough to hide it. But consider the possibility that God may want you to be more visible. He may have good reason for your work to be recognized, or your testimony to be shared. "God has placed the parts, each one of them, in the body just as He wanted" (1 Corinthians 12:18). Would you say no if he wanted you noticed?

LOOK AT IT THIS WAY

The purpose of the best man is simply to stand with the groom, to make sure all attention is riveted on him. The best man would be a fool if in the middle of the wedding processional, he suddenly turned to the wedding guests and began to sing a song or engage in a humorous monologue. The best man has fulfilled his purpose most admirably when he draws no attention to himself, but focuses all attention upon the bride and groom.

And that is what John did. If Jesus Christ was the groom, then the Baptizer was committed to being the best man and nothing else. That was the purpose that flowed from his call, and he had no desire to anything beyond. Thus to see the crowd headed toward Christ was all the affirmation John needed; his purpose had been fulfilled. "He must increase, but I must decrease," he said to those who had queried him about his attitude. What John had started out to accomplish—the introduction of Christ as the Lamb of God—had been accomplished. Having made the connection, John was satisfied and ready to withdraw.

—Gordon MacDonald

THE TRULY CHRISTIAN ATTITUDE IS TO NEITHER BE SEEKING THE SPOTLIGHT NOR SEEKING THE CORNER, BUT TO BE SEEKING THE PLACE GOD DESIRES FOR US. AND GIVING HIM THANKS WHEREVER THAT IS.

THE CENTURION
SUBMITTED TO AUTHORITY

SELECTIONS FROM MATTHEW 8

The doctors had done all they could. The prognosis was hopeless. His servant was dying. So the centurion's options had been whittled down to two. Cry out to Caesar and the Roman gods, or do something that seemed to have a better chance of working—find this Jesus!

When He entered Capernaum, a centurion came to Him, pleading with Him, "Lord, my servant is lying at home paralyzed, in terrible agony!... I am not worthy to have You come under my roof. But only say the word, and my servant will be cured. For I too am a man under authority, having soldiers under my command. I say to this one, 'Go!' and he goes; and to another, 'Come!' and he comes; and to my slave, 'Do this!' and he does it."

Hearing this, Jesus was amazed and said to those following Him, "I assure you: I have not found anyone in Israel with so great a faith!"... Then Jesus told the centurion, "Go. As you have believed, let it be done for you."

By connecting his observations on authority with their greater realities in the spiritual world, the centurion revealed a powerful tool in the workshop of Christian understanding: There is nothing that exists around us that doesn't have a deeper, more eternal meaning. Seeds becoming trees paint a picture of life after death. Geese flying in formation reflect an image of God's order. The things we see around us are much more than scenery. They're lenses for looking more closely at life.

LOOK AT IT THIS WAY

Do not be scared by the word *authority*. Believing things on authority only means believing them because you have been told them by someone you think trustworthy.

Ninety-nine percent of the things you believe are believed on authority. I believe there is such a place as New York. I have not seen it myself. I could not prove by abstract reasoning that there must be such a place. I believe it because reliable people have told me so. The ordinary man believes in the solar system, atoms, evolution, and the circulation of the blood on authority—because the scientists say so. Every historical statement in the world is believed on authority. None of us has seen the Norman Conquest or the defeat of the Armada. None of us could prove them by logic as you prove a thing in mathematics. We believe them simply because people who did see them have left writings that tell us about them: in fact, on authority. A man who jibbed at authority in other things as some people do in religion would have to be content to know nothing all his life.

—*C. S. Lewis*

GOD IS IN CHARGE OF THIS THING. AND WE CAN REST IN THE FACT THAT HIS AUTHORITY OVERRULES SIN, DEFEAT, AND HOPELESSNESS. LET HIM REIGN ON THE THRONE OF YOUR LIFE.

BARTIMAEUS
BELIEVING IN MIRACLES

SELECTIONS FROM MARK 10

He was making a scene, the kind that draws a stare, the kind that makes mothers grab their children by the hand and pull them close to their side. But the touch of God's hand was worth the risk of embarrassment. At least, that's the way blind Bartimaeus saw it.

As [Jesus] was leaving Jericho with His disciples and a large crowd, Bartimaeus (the son of Timaeus), a blind beggar, was sitting by the road. When he heard that it was Jesus the Nazarene, he began to cry out, "Son of David, Jesus, have mercy on me!" Many people told him to keep quiet, but he was crying out all the more, "Have mercy on me, Son of David!". . . He threw off his coat, jumped up, and came to Jesus.

Jesus answered him, "What do you want Me to do for you?"

"Rabbouni," the blind man told Him, "I want to see!"

"Go your way," Jesus told him. "Your faith has healed you." Immediately he could see and began to follow Him on the road.

We never know how we'll react in an emergency—to the blare of the siren, the whisk of the stretcher, the surprise of the late-night phone call. In moments of desperation, when we have nowhere else to turn, our reactions can run anywhere from panic to passive disbelief. But if God has been our source of refuge for even the minor scrapes of life, if he's been our first resort during the tiniest tremors of discomfort, then the big blows will only drive us where we've been all along—back on our knees.

LOOK AT IT THIS WAY

The cry had reached the ear of the Lord. He knew what the man wanted and was ready to grant it to him. But before he did it, he asked him, "What wilt thou that I should do to thee?" He wanted to hear not only the general petition for mercy, but the distinct expression of what the man's desire was that day. Until he verbalized it, he was not healed.

There are still petitioners to whom the Lord puts the same question who cannot get the aid they need until they answer that question. Our prayers must be a distinct expression of definite need, not a vague appeal to his mercy or an indefinite cry for blessing. It isn't that his loving heart does not understand or is not ready to hear our cry. Rather, Jesus desires such definite prayer for our own sakes because it teaches us to know our own needs better. Time, thought, and self-scrutiny are required to find out what our greatest need really is. Our desires are put to the test to see whether they are honest and real and are according to God's Word.

—Andrew Murray

YOUR BRAIN MAY TELL YOU DIFFERENTLY, YOUR FRIENDS MAY TELL YOU DIFFERENTLY, BUT WHEN YOU HONESTLY AND TRULY BELIEVE GOD FOR THE IMPOSSIBLE, ANYTHING CAN HAPPEN.

ZACCHAEUS
REPAYING FOR HIS SINS

SELECTIONS FROM LUKE 19

Little did the people of Jericho know that things were starting to look up the day Jesus caught sight of Zacchaeus in a sycamore tree. The wee little man with the grinch's heart was about to get a closer look at Jesus than he bargained for. Pass the tax refunds.

There was a man named Zacchaeus who was a chief tax collector, and he was rich. He was trying to see who Jesus was, but he was not able because of the crowd, since he was a short man. So running ahead, he climbed up a sycamore tree to see Jesus. . . .

When Jesus came to the place, He looked up and said to him, "Zacchaeus, hurry and come down, because today I must stay at your house." So he quickly came down and welcomed Him joyfully. All who saw it began to complain, "He's gone to lodge with a sinful man!" But Zacchaeus stood there and said . . . "Look, I'll give half of my possessions to the poor, Lord! And if I have extorted anything from anyone, I'll pay back four times as much!"

Restitution was an important biblical concept long before Zacchaeus inked his fingerprints on the pages of the New Testament. The Old Testament law required offenders to follow a two-step approach—restoring the value of the misused item or property to the rightful owner, as well as presenting a trespass offering to God on the altar. The message is clear. Guilt is never enough to right a wrong, and bitterness can leave behind a nasty build-up that hardens over the years. Is it pay-back time for something you've done?

LOOK AT IT THIS WAY

There are some people who do not believe in sudden conversions. I should like them to tell me when Zacchaeus was converted. He certainly was not converted when he went up into the sycamore tree; he certainly was converted when he came down. He must have been converted somewhere between the branches and the ground.

When a man begins to make restitution, it is a pretty good sign of conversion. Zacchaeus gave half his goods all at once, and he said, "If I have taken anything from any man, I restore him fourfold." I imagine the next morning, one of the servants of Zacchaeus going with a check for $1,000, and saying, "A few years ago, my master took from you wrongfully about $250, and this is restitution money." That would give confidence in Zacchaeus's conversion.

Unless our repentance includes conversion, it is not worth much. It's like pumping away continually at the ship's pumps without stopping the leaks. Prayer and confession are of no avail while we continue in sin.

−D. L. Moody

NICODEMUS
OVERCOMING CULTURE SHOCK

SELECTIONS FROM JOHN 3

Nicodemus knew his religion like the back of his hand. Ask him anything, and he'd at least give you an answer that sounded good. But this so-called Messiah was horning in on his territory, loosening the boards of a belief platform that Nicodemus had nailed down years ago.

There was a man from the Pharisees named Nicodemus, a ruler of the Jews. This man came to [Jesus] at night and said, "Rabbi, we know that You have come from God as a teacher, for no one could perform these signs You do unless God were with him." Jesus replied, "I assure you: Unless someone is born again, he cannot see the kingdom of God."

"But how can anyone be born when he is old?" Nicodemus asked Him. "Can he enter his mother's womb a second time and be born? . . . How can these things be?". . .

"If I have told you about things that happen on earth and you don't believe, how will you believe if I tell you about things of heaven?"

Many of us who shake our heads at our Sunday lawn-mowing neighbors while adjusting our neckties in the living room mirror need to check ourselves a little closer. Are we truly going to church to worship God? Or is that simply our culture of choice—like a patio breakfast with the Sunday paper is to the folks next door? Let's never get so caught up in our church culture—like the Pharisees in Nicodemus's day—that we miss the higher purpose of our faith. That's what our neighbors are really wanting to see.

LOOK AT IT THIS WAY

You must picture me alone in that room in Magdalen, night after night, feeling, whenever my mind lifted even for a second from my work, the steady, unrelenting approach of him whom I so earnestly desired not to meet. That which I greatly feared had at last come upon me.

In the Trinity Term of 1929, I gave in, and admitted that God was God: perhaps, that night, the most dejected and reluctant convert in all England. I did not then see what is now the most shining and obvious thing; the Divine humility which will accept a convert even on such terms. The Prodigal Son at least walked home on his own feet. But who can duly adore the Love which will open the high gates to a prodigal who is brought in kicking, struggling, resentful, and darting his eyes in every direction for a chance to escape? The words *compelle itrare*—compel them to come in—have been so abused; but, properly understood, they plumb the depth of the Divine mercy. The hardness of God is kinder than the softness of men, and his compulsion is our liberation.

—*C. S. Lewis*

THERE ARE UNSAVED PEOPLE WITHIN YOUR REACH WHO ARE STARTING TO SEE THE HOLES IN LIFE. THEY'RE ASKING QUESTIONS ONLY GOD HAS THE ANSWER TO. AND YOU'D BE A GREAT PERSON TO TELL THEM.

THOMAS
SEEING IS BELIEVING

SELECTIONS FROM JOHN 20

Thomas was a five-senses kind of guy trying to feel his way through a situation that made absolutely no sense. I mean, you just don't die one minute and then wake up seventy-two hours later as if nothing's happened. Who could believe a thing like that? Could you?

One of the Twelve, Thomas (called "Twin"), was not with them when Jesus came. So the other disciples kept telling him, "We have seen the Lord!" But he said to them, "If I don't see the mark of the nails in His hands, put my finger into the mark of the nails, and put my hand into His side, I will never believe!"

After eight days His disciples were indoors again, and Thomas was with them. Even though the doors were locked, Jesus came and stood among them. He said, "Peace to you!" Then He said to Thomas, "Put your finger here and observe My hands. Reach out your hand and put it into My side. Don't be an unbeliever, but a believer." Thomas responded to Him, "My Lord and my God!"

Carl Sagan once said he didn't want to believe; he wanted to know. He follows in a long line of the unsure and unsatisfied who don't understand that faith has a jumping-off place, and that the bold step from that precipice costs us the safety of our own assurances. It's not a trick implemented by a God who delights in watching people shiver on the high dive, but the far-sighted plan of a loving Father who longs for us to let him hold us in his arms after our first leap—and hear us ask if we can jump again.

LOOK AT IT THIS WAY

Thomas should have believed on the basis of the evidence he had from the other disciples and which was quite sufficient. Jesus said, "Because you have seen me, you have believed; blessed are those who have not seen and yet have believed." Is Jesus saying by this that believing is a blind leap of ungrounded faith? Quite the opposite! Because Thomas insisted on seeing and touching Jesus in his resurrected body, we have been given in the Gospels an even clearer evidence of the Resurrection than we would otherwise have had.

But Jesus is saying that Thomas should have believed without this additional evidence, because the evidence available to Thomas before was in itself sufficient. Before he saw Jesus, he was in the same position as we are today. Both he and we have the same sufficient witness of those who have seen and heard and who have had the opportunity to touch the resurrected Christ. In fact, in the light of this sufficient and sure witness, we, like Thomas, are disobedient if we do not bow. We are without excuse.

–Francis Schaeffer

BELIEVING IN JESUS IS REALLY AN EASY STEP, COMPLICATED ONLY BY THE NERVOUS PLEADINGS OF OUR OWN PRIDE AND FEAR. TAKE IT FROM THOMAS. HE ONLY WISHES HE'D HAVE DIVED IN SOONER.

JOSEPH OF ARIMATHEA
MEETING PRACTICAL NEEDS

SELECTIONS FROM LUKE 23

No one would have wanted Jesus' body to be tossed into a common grave with thieves and criminals. He'd been humiliated enough already. But everything had been so frightening, so sudden, so unbelievable. Nobody stopped to think about it. Well, almost nobody.

[Jesus] breathed His last. . . . All the crowds that had gathered for this spectacle, when they saw what had taken place, went home, striking their chests. But all who knew Him, including the women who had followed Him from Galilee, stood at a distance, watching these things.

There was a good and righteous man named Joseph, a member of the Sanhedrin, who had not agreed with their plan and action. He was from Arimathea, a Judean town, and was looking forward to the kingdom of God. He approached Pilate and asked for Jesus' body. Taking it down, he wrapped it in fine linen and placed it in a tomb cut into the rock, where no one had ever been placed.

There are so many little things we can do to show Christ's love to others—things so little, in fact, that we look right over their heads. But all it takes is a little thoughtfulness and a prayer for God's direction, and he can turn our smallest expressions into life-sized acts of ministry. It'll cost us some time we used to spend concentrating on our own busy schedules, our own problems, and our own concerns. But every minute we invest in trying to dream up new ways to serve God by serving others is time well spent.

LOOK AT IT THIS WAY

Slave is not a word most of us nowadays feel comfortable with. It is significant that most modern Bible translations use *servant* instead. For a slave is not his own, has no rights whatsoever, makes no choices about what he will do or how he is to serve.

Once we give up our slavery to the world, which is a cruel master indeed, to become Christ's bondslave, we live out our servitude to him by glad service to others. This volunteer slavery cannot be taken advantage of—we have chosen to surrender everything for love. It is a wholly different thing from forced labor. It is, in fact, the purest joy when it is most unobserved, most un-self-conscious, most simple, most freely offered.

Lord, free me to be your happy slave—to be the foot-washer of anyone today who needs his feet washed, his supper cooked, his faults overlooked, his work commended, his failure forgiven, his griefs consoled, or his button sewed on. Let me not imagine that my love for you is very great if I am unwilling to do for a human being something very small.

—Elisabeth Elliot

MAKE A POINT TO SAVE TEN MINUTES THIS WEEK JUST TO THINK ABOUT SOME WAYS YOU CAN SERVE YOUR FAMILY, YOUR CHURCH, YOUR FRIENDS IN NEED. DO IT PRACTICALLY ANYTIME.

PETER
CAPTURED BY CONSCIENCE

SELECTIONS FROM LUKE 22

Peter honestly didn't see it coming. Looking back, he's not even sure it would have mattered. He was just weakened by the fear, by the confusion, by the snap in Christ's voice after Peter had taken a sharp-edged swipe at that arresting officer. Could Jesus ever forgive him?

When they had lit a fire in the middle of the courtyard and sat down together, Peter sat among them. When a servant saw him sitting in the firelight, and looked closely at him, she said, "This man was with Him too." But he denied it: "Woman, I don't know Him!" After a little while, someone else saw him and said, "You're one of them too! . . . This man was certainly with Him, since he's also a Galilean." But Peter said, "Man, I don't know what you're talking about!"

Immediately, while he was still speaking, a rooster crowed. Then the Lord turned and looked at Peter. . . . And he went outside and wept bitterly.

There is guilt. And then there is conviction. Guilt depresses, defeats, demoralizes. Conviction motivates and redirects. Guilt is a seed planted strategically by the devil that crops up at the most unexpected times to remind us how pathetic we are. Conviction is an uncommon gift from the Holy Spirit that may come wrapped in sandpaper and burn all the way down. But its purpose is to redeem, to restore, to renew. Embrace conviction—sandpaper and all. It's God's patient way of giving us another chance.

LOOK AT IT THIS WAY

I think of Peter, who denied Jesus not once, but three times. How easy it would have been for Jesus to treat Peter bitterly, to make him feel as small as he had acted. But Jesus didn't say a word. Is that because Jesus understood how easy it is for us to betray even our best intentions when we're overwhelmed by insecurity and fear? Was that the brokenness Jesus saw in Peter?

Someone might suggest that surely there must have been cruelty in Jesus' eyes when "the Lord turned and looked straight at Peter." We all know those "looks that can kill." Had Jesus' glance been a look of cruelty, Peter might never have been salvaged. Instead, what Peter saw was a knowing look of disappointment: disappointment, because love hopes for the very best; knowing, because love recognizes human frailty. Isn't that the way God works in our own lives? No one loves us more. And he loves us despite the fact that he knows us inside out. Instead of rebuking us cruelly, he gives us that knowing look of disappointment—and calls us higher.

—F. LaGard Smith

GOD KNOWS HOW SICK YOU ARE OF THAT SAME OLD SIN. HE KNOWS HOW BADLY YOU WANT TO GET BEYOND IT. HE KNOWS IT'S MORE WEAKNESS THAN WICKEDNESS. AND HE'S HERE TO HELP YOU UP.

PETER
CONFIDENT IN CHRIST

SELECTIONS FROM ACTS 2

You'd hardly believe this was the same fellow who couldn't even stand up for Christ to a young local girl around the campfire the night they sentenced his Master to death. Listen to him now, though—fearlessly firing off the hard facts. You haven't heard the last of this guy.

Peter stood up with the Eleven, raised his voice, and proclaimed to them: ... "Let all the house of Israel know with certainty that God has made this Jesus, whom you crucified, both Lord and Messiah!"

When they heard this, they were pierced to the heart and said to Peter and the rest of the apostles: "Brothers, what must we do?"

"Repent," Peter said to them, "and be baptized, each of you, in the name of Jesus the Messiah for the forgiveness of your sins, and you will receive the gift of the Holy Spirit.". . . And with many other words he testified and strongly urged them, saying, "Be saved from this corrupt generation!"

Charles Spurgeon said that few of us have an adequate idea of what we may become—*even here on earth!*—by God's divine power and grace. We know one day we'll stand around the throne, with every pore in our being seeking a way to widen our praise. But if we just knew what he could do through us even now—with our pride beaten to a pulp, our doubt driven out the back door, our fear banished to the outfield. We can do all things—everything!—through him who gives us strength. Or were we just dreaming that?

LOOK AT IT THIS WAY

When God purposes to do something through you, the assignment will have God-sized dimensions. This is because God wants to reveal himself to you and to those around you. If you can do the work in your own strength, people will not come to know God. However, if God works through you to do what only he can do, you and those around you will come to know him. Jesus said, "He who does the truth comes to the light, that his deeds may be clearly seen, that they have been done in God" (John 3:21, NKJV).

When other people see you experiencing God, they are going to want to know how they, too, can experience God that way. Be prepared to point them to God. You will need to be very careful that any testimony about what God has done only gives glory to him. Pride may cause you to want to tell your experience because it makes you feel special. That will be a continuing tension. You must avoid any sense of pride. Therefore: "He who glories, let him glory in the Lord" (1 Corinthians 1:31, NKJV).

—Henry Blackaby

IF YOU'RE WORRIED ABOUT THE WAY YOUR WORDS WILL COME OUT, OR CONCERNED ABOUT THE IMPRESSION YOU'LL LEAVE BEHIND, GIVE GOD A CHANCE TO TAKE OVER. YOU WON'T HAVE A THING TO WORRY ABOUT.

PETER
CONFRONTING INDISCRETION

SELECTIONS FROM ACTS 5

One way of thinking says that Peter could have just let this whole thing go. After all, they did give a large offering to the church. How they arrived at the amount was their own business. But God's way of thinking said this was just the beginning. And he wanted it stopped. Now!

A man named Ananias, with Sapphira his wife, sold a piece of property. However, he kept back part of the proceeds with his wife's knowledge, and brought a portion of it and laid it at the apostles' feet.

Then Peter said, "Ananias, why has Satan filled your heart to lie to the Holy Spirit and keep back part of the proceeds from the field? Wasn't it yours while you possessed it? And after it was sold, wasn't it at your disposal? Why is it that you planned this thing in your heart? You have not lied to men but to God!"

When he heard these words, Ananias dropped dead, and a great fear came on all who heard.

The Bible says there's more than one potential danger that can come from having to rebuke a brother. Besides the risk of appearing superior or the threat of someone's self-defense kicking in to make matters even more uncomfortable, there's always the possibility that we may also be tempted (Galatians 6:1) to slacken our tolerance, to bend the Bible's teaching, to open our mind to the same kinds of seductions that have created the need for all this in the first place. "Watch yourself," the Word says. "Watch yourself."

LOOK AT IT THIS WAY

When General Norman Schwarzkopf was asked to define the secret of his success, he replied very simply, "I never walk past a problem." Another friend put it this way: "Just remember, when it comes to solving problems, the first price you pay is always the cheapest." We ignore problems, hoping they will go away, but that rarely happens. And the price of solving them goes up, not down.

Problems never get better when you ignore them. You may think you love someone too much to say anything. No, if you really loved him, you would speak the truth. You would speak it in love, but you would speak the truth he needed to hear. We are to love each other enough that we are willing for our brothers and sisters to hurt us if necessary.

Nobody wants to be hurt by his friends. We all want to be surrounded by people who will make us feel better about ourselves. But spiritual growth becomes possible when you let other people get close enough to you to say the things that you need to hear—whether you want to hear them or not.

—Ray Pritchard

CONFRONTATIONS OVER ISSUES OF MORALITY, MONEY, AND MORE ARE NEVER PLEASANT OR EASY. PRAY LONG AND HARD ABOUT WHAT GOD WANTS YOU TO DO. THIS IS SOMEONE'S LIFE YOU'RE DEALING WITH.

PETER
OVERCOMING PREJUDICE

SELECTIONS FROM ACTS 10

Peter's repugnance at the sight of unclean food was an automatic, ingrained reflex. But his response to God's interpretation—that Peter needed to get used to the fact that the dreaded Gentiles were moving into the covenantal neighborhood— was a sheer act of selfless surrender.

[Peter] saw heaven opened and an object coming down that resembled a large sheet being lowered to the earth by its four corners. In it were all the four-footed animals and reptiles of the earth, and the birds of the sky. Then a voice said to him, "Get up, Peter; kill and eat!"

"No, Lord!" Peter said. "For I have never eaten anything common and unclean!". . . The Spirit told him, "Three men are here looking for you. . . . Accompany them with no doubts at all.". . .

Peter said to them, "You know it's forbidden for a Jewish man to associate with or visit a foreigner. But God has shown me that I must not call any person common or unclean."

We may not consider ourselves prejudiced at all. Racial reconciliation is so out in the open today, the blinders slip off fairly easily. But there's more than other colors that can cause us to see people in a different light. What about the rich? Or the educated? The movie bug, the union man, the sports talk junkie? Whenever we group individuals into neat classifications and judge them against our own likes and dislikes, we run the risk of letting our preconceptions drive the way we react. And isn't that what prejudice is, after all?

LOOK AT IT THIS WAY

The story is told of two people sitting across a table from one another. There is food on their plates, but the silverware is too long for them to get the food to their own mouth. For both to eat, they have to feed the other. The white community can feed the black community repentance and blessings. The black community can feed the white community forgiveness, acceptance, and unconditional love. Both have something that each needs.

God is impressing his church to reconcile itself to the hurtful pain and prejudice of the past and to live in the truth that we are one in Christ. I am often asked what the church has lost and what it hopes to find. I believe what has been lost is the model for living like Christ and, in turn, reaching out to others, looking for opportunities to be a servant.

We will continue to be trapped in the issues of race and color as long as we have a mind-set based on cultural differences. Jesus shows us that you do not reach a nation with culture; you reach a nation with character, the character of Christ.

—Wellington Boone

HAS SOMETHING BEEN TELLING YOU TO OPEN YOURSELF TO THE POSSIBILITY OF YOUR OWN PREJUDICE? IT'S SUCH A SUBTLE SIN, IT'S SOMETIMES HARD TO SPOT. PRAY FOR A WAY TO MAKE SURE YOU'RE NOT INFECTED.

STEPHEN
THE ULTIMATE PRICE

SELECTIONS FROM ACTS 6 & 7

Stephen knew that their looks could kill. And he had good reason to think their stones wouldn't be far behind. What makes a man able to look his own death squarely in the eye—to brace for the pain, to stand by the confession that seals his fate? Only God knows.

Stephen, full of grace and power, was performing great wonders and signs among the people. Then some from what is called the Freedmen's Synagogue . . . stirred up the people, the elders, and the scribes; so they came up, dragged him off, and took him to the Sanhedrin. . . . They were enraged in their hearts and gnashed their teeth at him. . . . Then they screamed at the top of their voices, stopped their ears, and rushed together against him. They threw him out of the city and began to stone him. . . .

He called out: "Lord Jesus, receive my spirit!" Then he knelt down and cried out with a loud voice, "Lord, do not charge them with this sin!" And saying this, he fell asleep.

Stephen, though filled full of the Spirit, doesn't come off sounding like a natural-born troublemaker. He's not necessarily looking for a fight, just not willing to back down from one where his faith in Jesus is concerned. We don't have to be fearless firebrands to take a tough stand for Christ, only faithful soldiers who are willing to let God place us into situations that require the witness only we can give. The fire can get pretty hot, the looks can get pretty stony, but the Lord can keep us good and ready.

LOOK AT IT THIS WAY

When you hear about Christians being martyred for their faith, do you think of biblical figures such as Stephen or John the Baptist? If you do, you're out of date by a couple thousand years. In fact, more Christians were martyred for their faith in the twentieth century alone than in the previous nineteen centuries combined.

More than followers of any other faith, Christians around the world are suffering brutal persecution. Volume upon volume of irrefutable, documented evidence continues to surface, revealing horrifying atrocities increasingly being committed against those who dare to follow Jesus Christ. I wonder what God would do if all his people were on their knees begging for mercy for their persecuted brethren. Many things work against that kind of commitment. But with a crisis of this magnitude—blatant persecution—the consciences of Christians must be seared. May God grant that Christians who are so comfortable in freedom never consider prayer too great an effort, stay informed, and speak out in defense of those who are willing to pay the ultimate price for their faith.

—Chuck Colson

WHETHER YOU'RE IN PERSECUTED PLACES OF YOUR OWN OR WANTING TO HELP THOSE WHO ARE, REMEMBER TO PRAY. REMEMBER TO TRUST. REMEMBER THE MARTYRS.

PHILIP
SENSITIVE TO THE SPIRIT

SELECTIONS FROM ACTS 8

There's a language known only to the believer. Philip knew it. It's the language that resonates in a deep, hidden place about three buttons down your shirt and tells you something you have no logical way of knowing. It's the voice of the Spirit. Here's one who listened.

An angel of the Lord spoke to Philip: "Get up and go south to the road that goes down from Jerusalem to desert Gaza." So he got up and went.

There was an Ethiopian man, a eunuch and high official of Candace, queen of the Ethiopians, who was in charge of her entire treasury. He had come to worship in Jerusalem and was sitting in his chariot on his way home, reading the prophet Isaiah aloud. The Spirit told Philip, "Go and join that chariot." When Philip ran up to it, he heard him reading the prophet Isaiah, and said, "Do you understand what you're reading?". . . So Philip proceeded to tell him the good news about Jesus, beginning from that Scripture.

God cares about individuals. One of them works at the convenience market where you buy gas. You know him only from his nametag . . . as Matt. When you asked him why you hadn't seen him lately, he said he'd been to visit his grandfather, who's sick. "I'm sorry to hear that," you said. "Is he better now?" "No," he said. "They don't give him much time." A voice inside you says, *Why not ask Matt what he would do if he knew he only had a few days to live?* There's nobody behind you. You've got time. Stay sensitive.

LOOK AT IT THIS WAY

This story begins in the midst of an exciting revival. Bold Christians were proclaiming Christ from village to village. The Spirit of God was working. The atmosphere was electric. If you've ever been a part of a scene like this, you need no further explanation. If you haven't, you cannot imagine the excitement.

Suddenly, God steps in and does something strange. Without prior announcement—out of the clear blue—he dispatches an angel from heaven and redirects a man named Philip. How easy it would have been for Philip to be so caught up in the excitement and electricity of that Samaritan revival—where God was obviously at work—that he wasn't sensitive to a new direction. Not this man! He was alert and ready. Each day marked a new beginning. He had walked with God long enough to know that he has the right to throw a surprise curve—and often does!

Without stating his reason, without revealing the ultimate plan, God led Philip away from Samaria and out onto a desert road. The man was so sensitive to God's leading, there was no struggle.

—Charles Swindoll

THE BIGGEST HINDRANCE TO SPIRITUAL DEAFNESS (BESIDES WILLFUL SIN, OF COURSE) IS THE RACETRACK PACE OF LIFE. DO WHATEVER YOU HAVE TO DO IN ORDER TO GO SLOWLY ENOUGH TO HEAR GOD WHEN HE SPEAKS.

SIMON THE SORCERER
WANTING GOD SELFISHLY

SELECTIONS FROM ACTS 8

Simon was tuned in to the spirit world. You know, you don't have to be a Christian to have a flair for the mystical. So naturally he was intrigued by this Jesus worship. And especially the magic tricks His followers did. But he would soon find out it wasn't magic. It was serious.

A man named Simon had previously practiced sorcery in that city and astounded the Samaritan people, while claiming to be somebody great. . . . When Simon saw that the Holy Spirit was given through the laying on of the apostles' hands, he offered them money, saying, "Give me this power too, so that anyone I lay hands on may receive the Holy Spirit."

But Peter told him, "May your silver be destroyed with you, because you thought the gift of God could be obtained with money! . . . Repent of this wickedness of yours, and pray to the Lord that the intent of your heart may be forgiven you. For I see you are poisoned by bitterness and bound by iniquity."

When will we realize that the goose bumps are a bonus? They're not the main feature. When will we realize that our spiritual triumphs are not designed to impress our spiritual friends? They're to encourage the believer and attract attention (to God) from those he is seeking. The pull of pride and selfishness probably will never let up on us. But as we truly devote ourselves to God, as we genuinely seek his will, as we honestly confess that we want him to get the glory, he'll give us the strength to push the pull down.

LOOK AT IT THIS WAY

Today there is a trend toward increasing one's self-esteem. Consequently, we seem to be searching for a God who will help us feel okay about ourselves.

All this reminds me of "The Temple of the Thousand Buddhas," an unusual place of worship in Kyoto, Japan, where worshipers can literally design their own deity. The temple is filled with more than a thousand likenesses of Buddha—each one a little different from the next. Worshipers can pick and choose which they like best. Devotees of Buddha often try to find the likeness they feel most resembles themselves. Then they bow before it in worship.

Isn't this a bit like many churchgoers in our day? At the expense of reverence for his sovereignty, we have made God over into a pal who makes allowances for our sin and makes excuses for our backgrounds. There is a word to describe modifying God's laws like this—idolatry. The great Bible teacher Martyn Lloyd-Jones once wrote that people who teach that God is love without teaching that he hates sin are presenting another god—essentially Satan with a mask on.

–Greg Laurie

WE ALL POSSESS A TENDENCY TO WANT GOD FOR WHAT HE CAN DO FOR US. BUT REMEMBER TODAY THAT IF YOU'LL LET GOD USE YOU FOR WHAT HE WANTS, HE WILL MAKE SURE YOU GET TAKEN CARE OF.

ANANIAS
BELIEVING IN FORGIVENESS

SELECTIONS FROM ACTS 9

Ananias had good reason to be a little scared. Saul of Tarsus wasn't just your average convert— (if he really was converted) and with just the slightest wobble in his own spiritual perception, Ananias could be heading for a date with the dungeon. He's between God and a hard place.

In Damascus there was a disciple named Ananias. And the Lord said to him in a vision . . . "Get up and go to the street called Straight . . . to the house of Judas, and ask for a man from Tarsus named Saul, since he is praying there. In a vision he has seen a man named Ananias coming in and placing his hands on him so he may regain his sight."

"Lord," Ananias answered, "I have heard from many people about this man, how much harm he has done to Your saints in Jerusalem. And he has authority here from the chief priests to arrest all who call on Your name." But the Lord said to him, "Go! For this man is My chosen instrument."

You've seen him walk into church. The man whose wife and children have been coming by themselves for years. The man who reportedly told the preacher not to ever bother coming to visit him again—*ever!* Now he says he wants to become a Christian. People go down to shake his hand, but their smiles have that I'll-believe-it-when-I-see-it look, that see-if-he's-still-here-this-time-next-year look. He's not asking to be a deacon, for crying out loud. He just wants to give his life to Christ. Doesn't God do that here anymore?

LOOK AT IT THIS WAY

Let me think of the worst individual I know, the one for whom I have no affinity, the one who is a continual thorn in my flesh, who is as mean as can be; can I imagine that person being presented perfect in Christ Jesus?

It ought to be an easy thing for the Christian who thinks, to conceive of any and every kind of person being presented perfect in Christ Jesus, but how seldom do we think! If I am an earnest evangelical preacher, I may say to someone, "Oh, yes, I believe God can save you," while in my heart of hearts I don't believe there is much hope for him. Our unbelief stands as the supreme barrier to Jesus Christ's work in people's souls. But once let me get over my slowness of heart to believe in Jesus Christ's power to save, and I become a real generator of his power to others.

Are we banking in unshaken faith on the redemption, or do we allow men's sins and wrongs to so obliterate Jesus Christ's power to save that we hinder his reaching them?

—Oswald Chambers

ASK GOD TO GIVE YOU A NEW HEART FOR THE LOST— A HEART THAT BREAKS OVER MEN AND WOMEN WHO ARE REJECTING HIS LOVE AND KINDNESS, A HEART THAT BELIEVES IT WHEN GOD GETS THROUGH.

BARNABAS
ENCOURAGING OTHERS

SELECTIONS FROM ACTS 11

Barnabas is a smile and a pat on the back—a laugh that starts at his eyes and doesn't stop till the whole room is looking to see what's so funny. But he's the kind of friend who doesn't just tell you what you want to hear. You can tell that he really means it. That's Barnabas.

Those who had been scattered as a result of the persecution that started because of Stephen made their way as far as Phoenicia, Cyprus, and Antioch, speaking the message to no one except Jews. But there were some of them, Cypriot and Cyrenian men, who came to Antioch and began speaking to the Hellenists, proclaiming the good news about the Lord Jesus. . . .

The report about them reached the ears of the church in Jerusalem, and they sent out Barnabas to travel as far as Antioch. When he arrived and saw the grace of God, he was glad, and he encouraged all of them to remain true to the Lord with a firm resolve of the heart—for he was a good man, full of the Holy Spirit and of faith.

Encouragement takes time because encouragement is more than words. It's a lifestyle. It's a deliberate, watchful way of giving people the value God says they deserve, then blessing them with the wealth of your thoughtfulness. It works at church, at the job site, at the health club, at Little League practice—and it works best at home, where your spouse and children can feast on your kindnesses and genuine compliments. Encouragement is a gift you can start sharing today. Surely you know someone who's starved for some.

LOOK AT IT THIS WAY

The church is growing, and the Word is spreading like a flame. It's too big for the leaders to handle. Assistance is needed: gifted assistance. What does Barnabas do? He searches for and finds Saul of Tarsus, who was an outcast because of his former life. Not afraid to stick his neck out for a new Christian who was suspect in the eyes of the public, Barnabas took him by the hand and brought him to Antioch. Before the entire assembly, the "Son of Encouragement" gave his new friend a push into a priority position—in fact, it was into the very place where Barnabas himself had been experiencing remarkable blessing as a church leader.

Without a thought of jealousy, he later allowed Saul to take the leadership and set the pace for the first missionary journey. It is interesting to note that the names were soon switched from "Barnabas and Saul" to "Paul and Barnabas." It takes a great person to recognize that a man younger than he is has God-given abilities, and to encourage him to move ahead with full support. Oh, the need for this ministry!

—Charles Swindoll

IF YOU WANT TO MAKE SURE YOUR ENCOURAGEMENT DOESN'T COME OFF SOUNDING PHONY, THEN JUST MAKE SURE IT'S NOT. ASK GOD TO SHOW YOU HOW TO BE TRULY GLAD FOR OTHERS' SUCCESS.

THE PHILIPPIAN JAILER
ACCEPTING THE GOSPEL

SELECTIONS FROM ACTS 16

He could tell this was going to be no ordinary night at the lock-up from the very beginning. First, these prisoners wouldn't stop singing, then an earthquake rattled the doors off their hinges. Jailbreak! Pandemonium! And now he's just added a bazillion years to his life. Wow!

About midnight Paul and Silas were praying and singing hymns to God, and the prisoners were listening to them. Suddenly there was such a violent earthquake that the foundations of the jail were shaken, and immediately all the doors were opened, and everyone's chains came loose. When the jailer woke up and saw the doors of the prison open, he drew his sword and was going to kill himself, since he thought the prisoners had escaped. But Paul called out in a loud voice, "Don't harm yourself, because all of us are here!"

Then the jailer called for lights, rushed in, and fell down trembling before Paul and Silas. Then he escorted them out and said, "Sirs, what must I do to be saved?"

We should never get too business-as-usual about this amazing mystery. Every time someone says yes to God's saving message, the same blood that washed our sins down the drain of redemption flows across time and pours a brand new spirit into that person's life. Nor should we get so distant from the miracle of conversion that we only see its face from our seat on the church bench. It's the privilege of God's people to share this life-giving story with others and expect God to use our witness to win them over.

LOOK AT IT THIS WAY

Near the city of Sao José dos Campos, Brazil, is a remarkable facility. Twenty years ago, the Brazilian government turned a prison over to two Christians. The institution was renamed Humaita, and the plan was to run it on Christian principles. With the exception of two full-time staff, all the work is done by inmates. Chuck Colson visited the prison and made this report: "My guide escorted me to the notorious prison cell once used for torture. Today, he told me, that block houses only a single inmate. Slowly, he swung open the massive door, and I saw the prisoner in that punishment cell: a crucifix, beautifully carved by the Humaita inmates—the prisoner Jesus, hanging on a cross. 'He's doing time for the rest of us,' my guide said softly."

Christ has taken your place. There is no need for you to remain in the cell. Ever hear of a discharged prisoner who wanted to stay? Nor have I. When the doors open, the prisoners leave. The thought of a person preferring jail over freedom doesn't compute. Once the penalty is paid, why live under bondage?

—Max Lucado

COULD IT BE THAT YOU'RE NOT SO SURE YOU'VE TRULY ASKED CHRIST INTO YOUR HEART? HE'S A WHISPER AWAY, AND YOU'RE IN AS GOOD A PLACE AS ANY TO ASK HIM IN. SEE YOU 'ROUND THE THRONE.

APOLLOS & AQUILA
TEACHERS OF THE WORD

SELECTIONS FROM ACTS 18

The Hellenistic world had no shortage of teachers and philosophers who could expound on all the latest modes of thought and experience circulating around the Greek region. But there was a new brand of teacher in town. And his new textbook felt something like a sword.

A Jew named Apollos, a native Alexandrian, an eloquent man who was powerful in the Scriptures, arrived in Ephesus. This man had been instructed in the way of the Lord; and being fervent in spirit, he spoke and taught the things about Jesus accurately, although he knew only John's baptism. He began to speak boldly in the synagogue.

After Priscilla and Aquila heard him, they took him home and explained the way of God to him more accurately. . . . He greatly helped those who had believed through grace. For he vigorously refuted the Jews in public, demonstrating through the Scriptures that Jesus is the Messiah.

Bible teaching is so crucial to our lives. Even those who have been around the church for years—who have tried to give the Scriptures their close, regular attention—can still stumble over many doctrines and concepts. The answer is faithful Bible teaching, delivered by people who don't just exist to fill a Sunday morning hour but whose hearts breathe the Word, whose minds are enlightened to attract wisdom like a sponge, whose lives paint the pages in real-life colors. Is that what you should be doing? We sure need you.

LOOK AT IT THIS WAY

In order to be true to the Great Commission and to produce a mature church that would reproduce itself, the apostles knew they could not get sidetracked from their primary calling—to pray and to teach the Word of God.

It is not accidental that these believers were, first of all, continuing "steadfastly in the apostles' doctrine" or "teaching." It was the apostles' doctrine that gave direction to everything else that happened in the church in Jerusalem. Christian experience, both at the horizontal, human level (such as fellowship and sharing with each other) and at the vertical, divine level (such as prayer and praise) must have divine guidelines. Without these guidelines, Christians can get sidetracked onto peripheral issues and even depart from the will of God. For example, a Christ-centered community of love can quickly digress into a self-centered community. Therefore, all Christian experience must be rooted in and evaluated by Scripture. In this sense, continuing in the "apostles' doctrine" is foundational to all that we do in the church—and in life.

—Gene Getz

IF GOD HAS GRACED YOU WITH THE GIFT OF TEACHING, POUR YOUR HEART AND SOUL INTO IT. SOAK YOURSELF GOOD IN THE WORD EACH DAY. AND BRING IT HOME TO THE REST OF US WHERE OUR HEARTS CAN REALLY HEAR.

JULIUS
KINDNESS IN AN UNBELIEVER

SELECTIONS FROM ACTS 27

Paul's stormy journey across the sea to stand trial in Rome was made a bit more bearable by the kindness and concern of the Roman officer in charge of guarding him. Let's hope something of Paul's boldness and bravery rubbed off on Julius before his eternal ship ran aground.

When it was decided that we were to sail to Italy, they handed over Paul and some other prisoners to a centurion named Julius, of the Imperial Regiment. . . . The next day we put in at Sidon, and Julius treated Paul kindly and allowed him to go to his friends to receive their care. When we had put out to sea from there, we sailed along the northern coast of Cyprus because the winds were against us. . . .

When daylight came . . . they planned to run the ship ashore if they could. . . . The soldiers' plan was to kill the prisoners so that no one could swim off and escape. But the centurion kept them from carrying out their plan because he wanted to save Paul.

Christians don't hold the total market on kindness and concern. These qualities are gifts from God, and the unconverted who bear them simply don't realize they possess a shadow of God's character. But don't think that the he-was-such-a-good-person line will be a comfortable one to be carrying on the day when all men have to stand before the Judge of all the world. Kindness is great. It keeps the world from being as bad as it would be without God's grace. But it's a long way from enough to matter for very long.

LOOK AT IT THIS WAY

Niceness—wholesome, integrated personality—is an excellent thing. We must try by every medical, educational, economic, and political means in our power to produce a world where as many people as possible grow up "nice," just as we must try to produce a world where all have plenty to eat. But we must not suppose that even if we succeeded in making everyone nice, we should have saved their souls. A world of nice people, content in their own niceness, looking no further, turned away from God, would be just as desperately in need of salvation as a miserable world—and might even be more difficult to save.

For mere improvement is no redemption, though redemption always improves people even here and now, and will, in the end, improve them to a degree we cannot yet imagine. God became man to turn creatures into sons: not simply to produce better men of the old kind, but to produce a new kind of man. It is not like teaching a horse to jump better and better, but like turning a horse into a winged creature.

—*C. S. Lewis*

THANK GOD FOR THE KINDNESS HE HAS PLACED EVEN IN THE NON-CHRISTIANS AROUND US. BUT LET'S BE CAREFUL NOT TO LET THEIR COMPASSION CLOUD OUR AWARENESS OF THEIR NEED FOR JESUS CHRIST.

ONESIMUS
FROM USELESS TO USEFUL

SELECTIONS FROM PHILEMON

Onesimus had been the servant of one of Paul's pals, Philemon, but had robbed his master and headed for the border. Somewhere along the escape route, however, Jesus Christ had overtaken him and put him in contact with Paul, who writes back to Philemon to say...

I, Paul, as an elderly man and now also as a prisoner of Christ Jesus, appeal to you for my child, whom I fathered while in chains—Onesimus. Once he was useless to you, but now he is useful to both you and me. I am sending him—a part of myself—back to you. . . .

For perhaps this is why he was separated from you for a brief time, so that you might get him back permanently, no longer as a slave, but more than a slave—as a dearly loved brother. . . . So if you consider me a partner, accept him as you would me. . . . Since I am confident of your obedience, I am writing to you, knowing that you will do even more than I say.

Perhaps the greatest miracle of all is that the God who created all there is, who is ultimate perfection, who could choose anything or anyone to do his work—(or simply do it himself; if you want something done right, you know . . .)—still chooses to use US! If God himself has that much confidence in what he can do through us, how crazy are we to think that we can't do it, that we aren't any good, that we never will amount to anything? God has hand-picked us for his service. What are we waiting for?

LOOK AT IT THIS WAY

During the first ten years, I worried that my walk with the Lord wasn't good enough. Because I couldn't forget my past sins, I felt very guilty when I thought of all the grace he had shown me. During this time, I used to fall often and then get up again. It seemed that everything—even God—was against me, and that only faith was on my side. Sometimes it got so bad that I thought I was on my way to hell—willfully offending God—and that there was no salvation at all for me.

Thankfully, these worries did not weaken my faith in God, but actually made it stronger. When I finally reached the point where I expected the rest of my life to be very difficult, I suddenly found myself wholly changed. My soul, which had always been troubled, finally came to rest in a profound inner peace.

I consider God as my King, against whom I've committed all sorts of crimes. Confessing my sins to him and asking him to forgive me, I place myself in his hands to do whatever he pleases with me.

—Brother Lawrence

YOU'VE BEEN TRANSFORMED FROM SOMEONE LIMITED BY YOUR OWN POTENTIAL INTO SOMEONE WHO IS UNLIMITED BY GOD'S POTENTIAL. TRUST HIM TO ACCOMPLISH WHATEVER HE WANTS TO IN YOU.

PAUL
STRUGGLING WITH SIN

SELECTIONS FROM ROMANS 7

Paul was amazing. How many times have you heard it, or said it yourself—"I wish I could be like that Paul— his courage, his total devotion to Jesus Christ." But even Paul sometimes found himself in the vicious cycle of sin, slugging it out against his own flesh.

I know that nothing good lives in me, that is, in my flesh. For the desire to do what is good is with me, but there is no ability to do it. For I do not do the good that I want to do, but I practice the evil that I do not want to do. . . . So I discover this principle: when I want to do good, evil is with me.

For in my inner self I joyfully agree with God's law. But I see a different law in the parts of my body, waging war against the law of my mind and taking me prisoner to the law of sin in the parts of my body.

What a wretched man I am! Who will rescue me from this body of death? I thank God through Jesus Christ our Lord!

This is the place where we so often find ourselves— in the frustrating knot of sin and victory, failure and faithfulness, defeat and daring. We could kick ourselves for staying so susceptible to the tired yet tricky lines of the devil and our own propensity to sin. But like Paul so powerfully declares—even with the stench of his own sin around him—there's a way out of this mess. His name is Jesus Christ. And if we'll just take him at his word, we can find ourselves *off* this runaway roller coaster more often than we're *on* it.

LOOK AT IT THIS WAY

An old story is told of a dog sledder in Alaska who owned two dogs: one black and the other white. Once a month he would bring the dogs to town and pit them against one another, taking bets from the townspeople on which dog would win. Sometimes the white dog would be victorious; on other occasions the black dog would win. The fights were not fixed; in fact, they were quite ferocious—but the owner always bet on the winning dog. When he finally stopped fighting the animals, he was asked how he could always tell which dog would win. "That's easy," he replied. "The one I feed."

How do we win? How does the new nature conquer the old nature? How does the spirit overcome the flesh? We win in the battle of the mind. What are we feeding our mind? What are we watching? What are we reading? What are we listening to? What are we thinking of ? What does the landscape of our private world look like? We must be hungry for God— and for the goodness that a life with him yields.

—*Ed Young*

THANKS BE TO GOD. BY RECKONING OURSELVES AS DEAD TO SIN— THE POSITION WE'VE BEEN GIVEN BY BEING CRUCIFIED WITH CHRIST ON THE CROSS—WE CAN LOSE OUR INCLINATION FOR TEMPTATION.

PAUL
LOVE FOR HIS PEOPLE

SELECTIONS FROM ROMANS 9, 10, 11

The Jews weren't too crazy about Paul. After all, he had turned on them—gone over to the other side. But if those who opposed him would just listen to him, they'd see that his ministry to the Gentiles was designed to bring blessing to the Jewish people. Honest.

I could wish that I myself were cursed and cut off from the Messiah for the benefit of my brothers, my countrymen by physical descent. They are Israelites, and to them belong the adoption, the glory, the covenants, the giving of the law, the temple service, and the promises. . . .

Brothers, my heart's desire and prayer to God concerning them is for their salvation! . . . In view of the fact that I am an apostle to the Gentiles, I magnify my ministry, if I can somehow make my own people jealous and save some of them. For if their being rejected is world reconciliation, what will their acceptance mean but life from the dead?

Israel has a pivotal role in history. And Romans 9–11 paints a pretty clear picture of it. God originated his covenant with Israel—picked them out as his chosen people. But they rejected him—never more cruelly than when they crucified his only Son. As a result, God chose a people who once "were not a people" (1 Peter 2:10)—the Gentiles—grafting them into the original promises, with the express plan of making the Jews jealous enough for fellowship with God to one day return to the fold. And one day, in God's way, they will.

LOOK AT IT THIS WAY

Paul would be willing to undergo the greatest misery to do the Jews good. He would be content to be cut off from the land of the living, in the most shameful and ignominious manner. He would be content to be excommunicated from the society of the faithful, to be separated from the church, and from the communion of saints, as a heathen man and a publican, if that would do them good. He could wish himself no more remembered among the saints, his name blotted out of the church records; though he had been so great a planter of churches and the spiritual father of so many thousands, yet he would be content to be disowned by the church, cut off from the communion of it, and have his name buried in oblivion or reproach for the good of the Jews.

We ought to be in a special manner concerned for the spiritual good of our relations, our brethren, and kinsmen. To them we lie under special engagements, and we have more opportunity of doing good to them, and our usefulness to them we must in a special manner give account.

–Matthew Henry

PAUL LOVED HIS PEOPLE, HAD GREAT RESPECT FOR HIS HERITAGE. AND AS YOU STUDY, WATCH, AND GET TO KNOW THE JEWISH PEOPLE, YOU'LL LOVE THEM TOO. THEY ARE OUR FOREFATHERS IN THE FAITH.

PAUL
LOVE FOR THE CHURCH

SELECTIONS FROM 1 THESSALONIANS 2

Paul poured his life into the church. His relationship with the many churches he started and sustained was like a father for his children—or, as he said, like a mother: "Again I am in the pains of childbirth for you until Christ is formed in you." There's a lot of love in this passage.

We cared so much for you that we were pleased to share with you not only the gospel of God but also our own lives, because you had become dear to us. For you remember our labor and hardship, brothers. Working night and day so that we would not burden any of you, we preached God's gospel to you. . . .

As you know, like a father with his own children, we encouraged, comforted, and implored each one of you to walk worthy of God, who calls you into His own kingdom and glory. . . . For who is our hope, or joy, or crown of boasting in the presence of our Lord Jesus at His coming? Is it not you? For you are our glory and joy!

The thought of a serious believer existing outside the blessings and boundaries of the church is a lie in the language of Christian living. God's people are grown to live in relationship, feeding off their gospel fellowship, partaking of the sacred reminders of the Christian mystery, lifting each other up in believing prayer, and holding each other accountable as witnesses for Christ. Love your church. Serve your church. Minister to the needy. Invest yourself in its mission, and find your role in helping bring it to pass.

LOOK AT IT THIS WAY

The church is the body of believers, not the building where the believers assemble. It is the group with whom we marry our children, bury our dead, receive comfort in crisis, accept meals in sickness, partake of the Lord's Supper, learn about the character of God, become trained in doctrine, commune with Christ, fellowship with other believers, become discipled in the way we should walk, develop a personal ministry, honor God with our tithes and offerings, bring unsaved friends, hear the preaching of God's Word, express our spiritual gifts, raise our children in spiritual instruction, and take vows for which we are accountable.

Have you ever really considered the depth of the role your church plays in your life and the life of your family? A great need today is that Christians revalue the church—that they recognize the importance of membership in a vital body of believers. Supporting a local church through membership—not merely attendance—represents the most significant of the public spiritual disciplines. If we truly love Christ, we will want to be around his people.

—Patrick Morley

IF YOU'RE NOT ACTIVELY INVOLVED IN A CHURCH, IT'S TIME YOU FOLLOWED GOD'S CALL TO THE ONE WHERE HE WANTS YOU. TAKE IT FROM THOSE WHO ARE ALREADY THERE. YOU'LL LOVE IT.

PAUL
NO LONE RANGER

SELECTIONS FROM TITUS 1 & 3

As capable and in-charge as Paul was, he never succumbed to the debilitating mistake of taking too much on himself. His habit of sharing the responsibilities of ministry with a trusted team of leaders shows up in nearly all his books. Like in this one, to Titus.

Titus, my true child in our common faith . . . The reason I left you in Crete was to set right what was left undone and, as I directed you, to appoint elders in every town. . . .

When I send Artemas to you, or Tychicus, make every effort to come to me in Nicopolis, for I have decided to spend the winter there. Diligently help Zenas the lawyer and Apollos on their journey, so that they will lack nothing. And our people must also learn to devote themselves to good works for cases of urgent need, so that they will not be unfruitful.

All those who are with me greet you. Greet those who love us in the faith. Grace be with all of you.

Beyond our hunger for having fellowship with those inside our own churches, we need to draw our lines big enough to take in all those who embrace the Christian faith. If we keep ourselves too sequestered from other expressions of worship and other methods of fulfilling our shared priorities, we'll find ourselves plowing the same ground, wasting many of our efforts, and—worse!—growing a little bit competitive with those we're supposed to be on the same side with. We're all in this thing together, aren't we?

LOOK AT IT THIS WAY

Many men have a Lone Ranger mentality. They live with the belief that they can right the wrongs, beat the world into submission, be successful at everything— and never need anyone's help along the way. The mask they wear is the mask of denial. The silver bullets they roll in their fingers are engraved with the word *egotist*.

When Jesus sent the disciples out on their first short missionary journey, he sent them two by two. It wasn't to get better hotel rates or to have argumentative advantage in the sharing of their faith. It was for mutual support and encouragement when things were not going well. He did not want them to be alone in the calling to follow him. When the apostle Paul traveled on his missionary journeys planting churches, he brought others along for support, help, and encouragement. Both Paul and Jesus demonstrated the call of the gospel as the call to friendship, like-mindedness, and a supportive community. God has created us to hunger for relationships. When we deny that hunger, we endanger our own emotional and spiritual well-being.

—Jim Smoke

PAUL
EMBRACING HARDSHIP

SELECTIONS FROM 2 CORINTHIANS 4 & 11

Unbelievable. What this one man endured for the cause of Christ is beyond most of our imaginations. Lashes, rods, beatings, hunger. Imprisonment, courtrooms, shipwreck, threats. One thing's for sure as we read his letters: This guy believed what he professed.

Five times I received from the Jews 40 lashes minus one. Three times I was beaten with rods. Once I was stoned. Three times I was shipwrecked. I have spent a night and a day in the depths of the sea. On frequent journeys, I faced dangers from rivers, dangers from robbers, dangers from my own people, dangers from the Gentiles, dangers in the city, dangers in the open country, dangers on the sea, and dangers among false brothers. . . .

All this is because of you, so that grace, extended through more and more people, may cause thanksgiving to overflow to God's glory. Therefore we do not give up. . . . We do not focus on what is seen, but on what is unseen.

Paul was on a mission, a crusade for Christ. There's something about throwing your whole self into a mighty cause that almost feeds off adversity. More often then not, though, our hardships don't come with such clear reasons or instructions. Yet we know that whatever we face has a benefit buried just beneath the surface. Or it can be transformed into having a benefit by the God who never allows us to endure more than we can stand. Embrace your hardship as something you can grow from. And let God perform his perfect work.

LOOK AT IT THIS WAY

Acceptance of a share, still more the willing acceptance of more than our full share, in the tragedy of life is positive; it has about it something vitalizing. Those who meet pain clear-eyed, and with a positive and active acceptance, who "face the music" as the slang phrase has it; those who are not only ready to do their bit, but to share their bit in the world's sorrow, make a great discovery. They find not only that they are enabled to bear their sorrow in a way which hurts less (for that which hurts most in the bearing is that which is most resented; what is most freely accepted hurts least)—but that they achieve an enrichment and a growth in personality which makes them centers of influence and light, in ways of which they never suspected the possibility.

Few things can so inspire and re-create the human heart as the spectacle of crushing misfortune cheerfully and heroically borne; and the unconscious influence which those exert is far greater than they or others comprehend. Suffering lightly borne is constructive work, for pain conquered is power.

—Lily Dougall

THE HARDEST SUFFERING TO ENDURE IS THE SUFFERING THAT SEEMS TO MAKE NO SENSE. BUT TRUST THAT GOD HAS MADE SENSE OF IT. AND THAT HE WILL SEE YOU THROUGH TO A BETTER END.

PAUL
HUMBLE BEFORE GOD

SELECTIONS FROM 1 TIMOTHY 1

Paul's natural demeanor was one of cold, calculating efficiency. Today, we'd call him driven. But God had thrown a huge bucket of grace onto the hot coals of his tough-minded temper, and now his hard-driving focus was getting to share space with a calm, gracious humility.

I give thanks to Christ Jesus our Lord, who has strengthened me, because He considered me faithful, appointing me to the ministry— one who was formerly a blasphemer, a persecutor, and an arrogant man. Since it was out of ignorance that I had acted in unbelief, I received mercy, and the grace of our Lord overflowed, along with the faith and love that are in Christ Jesus. . . .

"Christ Jesus came into the world to save sinners"—and I am the worst of them. But I received mercy because of this, so that in me, the worst of them, Christ Jesus might demonstrate the utmost patience as an example to those who would believe in Him for eternal life.

Humility before God is a long way from weak-in-the-knees bowing and scraping. There'll come a time for that—for those who choose to wait until humility is forced upon them. But being humble right now means accepting God's picture of us as the real one—our sins covered by Christ's forgiveness, our heart filled with his Spirit, our will emboldened by the power of Christ's resurrected glory. It's imagining, as Max Lucado says, that if God carried a wallet, he'd have our picture in it. How do we say thank-you for that?

LOOK AT IT THIS WAY

There are those who exhibit a Pharisaic holiness; they thank God with an arrogant offensiveness that they are not as other men are; they have forgotten the horrible pit and miry clay from where they were taken. A holy man is not one who has his eyes set on his own whiteness but one who is personally and passionately devoted to the Lord who saved him—one whom the Holy Spirit takes care shall never forget that God has made him what he is by sheer sovereign grace.

The humility Paul manifests was produced in him by the remembrance that Jesus, whom he had scorned and despised, whose followers he had persecuted, whose church he had harried, had not only forgiven him, but had made him his chief apostle. Show such a servant of God the backslider, the sinner steeped in the iniquity of our cities, and there will spring up in his heart an amazing well of compassion and love for that one, because he himself has experienced the grace of God that goes to the uttermost depths of sin and lifts to the highest heights of salvation.

—Oswald Chambers

TAKE SOME TIME TODAY TO REFLECT AGAIN ON THE BEAUTY OF YOUR SALVATION— REMEMBERING THE PRICE, RECAPTURING THE REALITY, RESTORING THE JOY. IT'S A GREAT DAY TO BE HUMBLE.

PAUL
IN THE NEED OF PRAYER

SELECTIONS FROM PAUL'S LETTERS

Paul under-stood that his success in ministry had a direct correla-tion with the prayers of the saints. He begged for prayer, pleaded for prayer, expected some-thing from prayer—not so that he could get blessings from God, but so that God could share his blessings through him.

Brothers, pray for us. . . . Pray also for me, that the message may be given to me when I open my mouth to make known with bold-ness the mystery of the gospel. For this I am an ambassador in chains. Pray that I might be bold enough in Him to speak as I should. . . .

Finally, pray for us, brothers, that the Lord's message may spread rapidly and be honored, just as it was with you, and that we may be delivered from wicked and evil men, for not all have faith. . . . You can join in helping with prayer for us, so that thanks may be given by many on our behalf for the gift that came to us through the prayers of many.

The prayers of others on our behalf can become a forgotten piece of our spiritual arsenal. We do without them because we don't want to bother anyone. And even when we ask someone for prayer, we often doubt that their I'll-be-praying-for-you's will ever be acted upon. (We know, at least, that we've failed to do it for others.) Until we believe that prayers are more than a duty, more than comforting thoughts and wish lists but a mighty force of spiritual dynamite, we'll keep running on empty. We'll keep ignoring the promise.

LOOK AT IT THIS WAY

Satan's desire is to destroy the work of Christ in the world. One of his most effective ways of doing that is to destroy pastors. If Satan can bring them down, causing disgrace and ridicule to taint the work of Christ, the nonbelieving world will not be attracted to Jesus. We have all seen the carnage left around us as pastors have failed morally or have simply left the ministry because of disillusionment.

Pastors need to know their churches are with them and are praying for them, so they can be emboldened to share the whole counsel of God and not cower in the face of opposition within or without the church.

E. M. Bounds said it this way: "The men in the pew given to praying for the pastor are like poles which hold up the wires along which the electric current runs. They are not the power, neither are they the specific agents in making the Word of the Lord more effective. But they hold up the wires upon which the divine power runs to the hearts of men. They make conditions favorable for the preaching of the Gospel."

–Dale Schlafer

YOU DEPEND ON OTHER'S PRAYERS MUCH MORE THAN YOU KNOW, JUST AS THEY DEPEND ON YOURS FOR THEIR GODLY POWER AND STRENGTH. FIND SOMEONE YOU KNOW WHO WILL PROMISE TO PRAY.

JOHN
APPEALING FOR LOVE

SELECTIONS FROM 2 JOHN

John was known as the apostle Jesus loved. And love set the tone for his legacy. He had discovered the secret of Christian living, the unifying bond between different classes of people— the mark that would distinguish the church in the world. Love. Love never fails.

To the elect lady and her children, whom I love in truth—and not only I, but also all who have come to know the truth— because of the truth that remains in us and will be with us forever. Grace, mercy, and peace will be with us from God the Father and from Jesus Christ, the Son of the Father, in truth and love. . . .

I urge you, lady—not as if I were writing you a new command, but one we have had from the beginning—that we love one another. And this is love: that we walk according to His commands. This is the command as you have heard it from the beginning: you must walk in love.

Love is the most unnatural of the virtues. Perhaps that's why God has earmarked it as the defining characteristic of his people. It must fight every shred of self; it must quiet every shout of discord. It can only be truly fashioned in people who have been made unnatural themselves, who have been transformed into new creatures. So love is our mark. Love will still remain after faith has finally seen its object, after hope has finally held its reward. Love will last forever because it is being grown in the people who will live forever.

LOOK AT IT THIS WAY

Though natural likings should normally be encouraged, it would be quite wrong to think that the way to become charitable is to sit trying to manufacture affectionate feelings. Do not waste time bothering whether you "love" your neighbor; act as if you did. As soon as we do this, we find one of the great secrets. When you are behaving as if you loved someone, you will presently come to love him.

If you injure someone you dislike, you will find yourself disliking him more. If you do to him a good turn, not to please God and obey the law of charity, but to show him what a fine forgiving chap you are, and to put him in your debt, and then sit down to wait for his "gratitude," you will probably be disappointed. (People are not fools: they have a very quick eye for anything like showing off or patronage.) But whenever we do good to another self, just because it is a self, made (like us) by God, and desiring its own happiness as we desire ours, we shall have learned to love it a little more.

—C. S. Lewis

LOVE DRAWS YOU ABOUT AS CLOSE TO THE HEART OF GOD AS YOU CAN GET. YOU'LL PROBABLY FACE A SITUATION TODAY THAT WILL GIVE YOU THE OPTION OF USING IT—AND LETTING YOU SEE FOR YOURSELF.

JOHN
OPEN TO GOD'S REVELATION

SELECTIONS FROM REVELATION 1

Stranded on the island of Patmos, about as far away as he could be from everything he'd ever known, John never thought he'd be used by God again. But he continued taking time on the Lord's Day to meet with God in worship. And one day, something unbelievable happened.

I, John, your brother and partner in the tribulation, kingdom, and perseverance in Jesus, was on the island called Patmos because of God's word and the testimony about Jesus. I was in the Spirit on the Lord's day, and I heard behind me a loud voice like a trumpet saying, "Write on a scroll what you see." . . .

I turned to see the voice that was speaking to me. When I turned I saw seven gold lampstands, and among the lampstands was One like the Son of Man. . . . When I saw Him, I fell at His feet like a dead man. He laid His right hand on me, and said, "Don't be afraid! . . . Write what you have seen, what is, and what will take place after this."

Even when I am old and gray, God, do not abandon me. Then I will proclaim Your power to another generation, Your strength to all who are to come" (Psalm 71:18). The cry of the psalmist, longing to be used until his dying breath, seeing the lasting importance of passing down a godly heritage to his children and grandchildren, reveals the kind of heart we all should have. Even when we're old and gray, Lord, use us. Keep us open. Keep us right where you want us to be.

LOOK AT IT THIS WAY

All of us are faced with two realms of reality. We deal with the visible, the tangible every day. We know that it is real. But there is another world, another realm of reality which vies for our attention. The spiritual, the heavenly, and the eternal! The door which John saw open was the door between earth and heaven, the aperture between the visible reality and the invisible reality.

Amid all that bids you run and hide and flounder in hopelessness, don't you see that same open door? Don't you hear that same thunderous voice bidding you to come and see? Don't you see that throne and He who sits upon it? He is not wringing His hands over a world catapulting into oblivion. He does not walk around the throne with furrowed brow and worried look. He is the Sovereign God. He is running the show! Get your philosophy of history in line with that, and you will be prepared to praise. Repent of the sin of believing that things are as they appear to be. Ask God to reshape your whole perspective around the vision of God on a throne.

—Jack Taylor

MAKE IT YOUR GOAL IN OLD AGE TO KEEP YOUR EAR TUNED MORE SHARPLY TO GOD'S VOICE, FOLLOWING HIM FAITHFULLY ALL THE WAY TO THE END. THIS IS A LIFETIME DEAL. NO QUITTERS NEED APPLY.

SOURCES

PAGE   CONTRIBUTOR, TITLE, AND PUBLISHER

9   Lawrence F. Burtoft, *Reclaiming the Culture* (Focus on the Family)

11   Oswald Chambers, *My Utmost for His Highest* (Barbour)

13   Andrew Murray, *Daily Secrets of Christian Living* (Kregel)

15   Gene Getz, *Men of Character: Abraham* (Broadman & Holman)

17   C. Welton Gaddy, *A Love Affair with God* (Broadman & Holman)

19   Tom Sirotnak, *Ultimate Warriors* (Broadman & Holman)

21   Chip Ricks, *The Plans of His Heart* (Broadman & Holman)

23   Josh McDowell, *The Father Connection* (Broadman & Holman)

25   Henry Blackaby, *Experiencing God* (Broadman & Holman)

27   James R. Lucas, *Walking Through the Fire* (Broadman & Holman)

29   Charles Swindoll, *Man to Man* (Zondervan)

31   Charles Spurgeon, *Morning and Evening* (Hendrickson)

33   John Maxwell, *The Success Journey* (Nelson)

35   Charles Stanley, *The Wonderful Spirit-Filled Life* (Nelson)

37   John Eldredge, *Reclaiming the Culture* (Focus on the Family)

39   Matthew Henry, *A Commentary on the Whole Bible* (Revell)

41   L. H. Hardwick, Jr., sermon preached at Christ Church, Nashville,
        June 22, 1997 (used with permission)

43   Greg Laurie, *The Great Compromise* (Word)

45   Joe Wright, quoted in *Basic Training* (Nelson)

47   Gene Getz, *Men of Character: Joshua* (Broadman & Holman)

49   C. W. Brister, *Dealing with Doubt* (Broadman & Holman)

51   Dietrich Gruen, *Fathers Who Made a Difference* (Bethany House)

53   O. S. Hawkins, *Moral Earthquakes* (Broadman & Holman)

55   William Law, *A Practical Treatise upon Christian Perfection* (public domain)

57   Charles Spurgeon, *A Passion for Holiness in a Believer's Life* (Emerald)

59   Millard MacAdam, *Intentional Integrity* (Broadman & Holman)

61   Jim Henry, *Keeping Life in Perspective* (Broadman & Holman)

63   Gene Getz, *Men of Character: David* (Broadman & Holman)

65   Robert Webber, *Blended Worship* (Hendrickson)

67   Oswald Chambers, *Conformed to His Image* (Discovery House)

69   Charles Spurgeon, *A Passion for Holiness in a Believer's Life* (Emerald)

71   Charles Swindoll, *David* (Word)

73   Gary Smalley and John Trent, *The Blessing* (Pocket Books)

75   Donald Whitney, *Spiritual Disciplines for the Christian Life* (NavPress)

77   Ray Pritchard, *The ABCs of Wisdom* (Moody)

SOURCES

SOURCES

PAGE   CONTRIBUTOR, TITLE, AND PUBLISHER

149   Ray Pritchard, *The ABCs of Wisdom* (Moody)
151   Wellington Boone, *Breaking Through* (Broadman & Holman)
153   Chuck Colson, foreword from *In the Lion's Den* (Broadman & Holman)
155   Charles Swindoll, *Strengthening Your Grip* (Word)
157   Greg Laurie, *The Great Compromise* (Word)
159   Oswald Chambers, *Conformed to His Image* (Discovery House)
161   Charles Swindoll, *Growing Strong in the Seasons of Life* (Multnomah)
163   Max Lucado, *In the Grip of Grace* (Word)
165   Gene Getz, *The Walk* (Broadman & Holman)
167   C. S. Lewis, *Mere Christianity* (Macmillan)
169   Brother Lawrence, *The Practice of the Presence of God* (Whitaker)
171   Ed Young, *Been There, Done That, Now What?* (Broadman & Holman)
173   Matthew Henry, *A Commentary on the Whole Bible* (Revell)
175   Patrick Morley, *Seven Seasons of a Man's Life* (Nelson)
177   Jim Smoke, *How a Man Measures Success* (Bethany House)
179   Lily Dougall, quoted in *Salute to a Sufferer* (Abingdon)
181   Oswald Chambers, *Conformed to His Image* (Discovery House)
183   Dale Schlafer, *Seven Promises of a Promise Keeper* (Focus on the Family)
185   C. S. Lewis, *Mere Christianity* (Macmillan)
187   Jack Taylor, *The Hallelujah Factor* (Broadman & Holman)

87 - The passion to Finish   * p. 89

MORE DEVOTIONAL READING

If you liked this book, there are plenty more
One Minute Bible™ devotional collections:

Men in Leadership
0-8054-9153-8

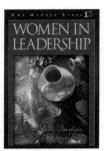

Women in Leadership
0-8054-9193-7

**90 Days with the
Christian Classics**
0-8054-9278-X

**90 Days in the Word for
Business Professionals**
0-8054-9363-8

Starting Today
0-8054-3780-0

Women of Character
0-8054-2686-8